Advance Praise

"The *Flourish* Series will never, ever leave the top of my desk; it is a comprehensive guide for life. Its insight and organization are amazing. I don't know how one person could compose the whole world of what is right. I am looking forward to following the path of this masterpiece."

—**Dr. Story Musgrave**, surgeon, Marine veteran, six-time NASA astronaut, and Hubble Space Telescope repairman, Kissimmee, Florida

"Bold, monumental, brilliant, and provocative. Bitz insightfully nails how America has lost its way and offers thoughtful solutions to find our way back. A courageous and important series."

—**Bob Vanourek**, award-winning author and former CEO of five firms, Cordillera, Colorado

"*Toward Truth, Freedom, Fitness, and Decency* is an extraordinary study . . . as compelling a read as it is thoughtful and thought-provoking . . . Very highly recommended for both community and academic library collections and . . . for students, political activists, and ordinary folk interested in the social, cultural, economic, and political issues that so trouble our country today."

—**Susan Bethany**, *Midwest Book Review*, Oregon, Wisconsin

"The *Flourish* Series are two of the most important books that I have ever read. They are a badly-needed articulation of the problems besetting our country and the solutions to them. Anyone who reads these books will benefit from them, and they are a vital read for all the conscientious people who want what's best for future generations, and not just what's best for themselves."

—**Gary Fenchuk**, award-winning developer, CEO, and author of *Timeless Wisdom*, Midlothian, Virginia

"I am absolutely blown away by Mark's fact-based analysis and suggested remedies on such a huge scale. A tremendous series and worthy of careful reading."

—**Paul de Lima**, former CEO and owner of Paul de Lima Coffee, Syracuse, New York

"The *Flourish* Series provides a road map for living a useful, happy and healthy life. I love it. It should be mandatory reading for every high school student."

—**Mitch Sill**, retired CEO and owner of Road Machinery & Supplies Co., Duluth, Minnesota

"Mark has written clearly and truthfully, a complete Operator's Manual for Life. I will share the series with those who are dearest to me."

—**Haisook Somers**, mother, award-winning maple syrup producer, philanthropist, and volunteer, Montreal, Quebec

"I am profoundly impressed with the *Flourish* Series. Mark has delineated and backed up with facts and thoughtful analysis timeless truths and behaviors that will help many individuals lead more fulfilled lives. His work could not come at a better time. As fewer people learn these truths and behaviors from their families and faiths, an insightful, well-organized, secular expression of them becomes ever more important."

—**John Doyle**, owner and CEO of Doyle Security Systems, Rochester, New York

"Every chapter is worth reading and pondering."

—**Richard Kaufman**, chair of Amstore Corporation, Chicago, Illinois

"Mark blends his considerable experience to design a plan for America to not only grow but also to flourish. His practical and commonsense plan is a must read for all thinking Americans."

—**Carl Youngman**, former CEO of more than twenty companies, Boston, Massachusetts

"Mark delves into some of our country's biggest challenges and cuts through the politics. He takes you beyond the approaches of the right or the left and presents creative and practical winning ones."

—**Stephen McConnell**, president of Solano Ventures, Scottsdale, Arizona

"I find myself staring off into space and pondering Mark's ideas. I agree with what he says, and I am pleased to find so much well-synthesized and organized thought in one treatise."

—**Tom Ewert**, retired federal judge, Naples, Florida

"The *Flourish* Series is thought-provoking and thoroughly interesting. It examines many of our country's challenges and offers a comprehensive set of solutions. It is incredibly innovative and has stimulated many discussions among our family and friends. The books are a must-read for our country's leaders and those who are concerned about it."

—**Mark Danni**, artistic director, Theatre Zone, and president of Karemar Productions, Naples, Florida

"Wow! The *Flourish* Series is comprehensive and very thought-provoking. It will encourage many a vigorous debate around the kitchen table."

—**Carole-Ann Miller**, CEO, Camsa, Inc., Halifax, Canada

"Even though I have a more biblical viewpoint of the world, the teaching and wisdom of the *Flourish* Series should be mandatory reading for all first-year college students."

—**Kenneth Lockard**, founder of numerous companies, CEO of Lockard Companies, Cedar Falls, Iowa

Toward Truth,

Freedom, Fitness,

and Decency

SECOND EDITION

FLOURISH

Toward Truth, Freedom, Fitness, and Decency

MARK W. BITZ

GREENLEAF
BOOK GROUP PRESS

This publication is designed to provide accurate and authoritative information in regard to the subject matter covered. It is sold with the understanding that the publisher and author are not engaged in rendering legal, accounting, or other professional services. If legal advice or other expert assistance is required, the services of a competent professional should be sought.

Published by Greenleaf Book Group Press
Austin, Texas
www.gbgpress.com

Copyright ©2018 Mark W. Bitz

Distributed by Greenleaf Book Group

For ordering information or special discounts for bulk purchases, please contact Greenleaf Book Group at PO Box 91869, Austin, TX 78709, 512.891.6100.

Design and composition by Greenleaf Book Group
Cover design by Greenleaf Book Group
Cover image: ©iStockphoto.com/pro_

Cataloging-in-Publication data is available.

Print ISBN: 978-1-62634-525-6

eBook ISBN: 978-1-62634-526-3

Audiobook ISBN: 978-1-62634-527-0

Part of the Tree Neutral® program, which offsets the number of trees consumed in the production and printing of this book by taking proactive steps, such as planting trees in direct proportion to the number of trees used: www.treeneutral.com

TreeNeutral

Printed in the United States of America on acid-free paper

18 19 20 21 22   10 9 8 7 6 5 4 3 2 1

Second Edition

So you and future generations may realize
your full potential and do better than we have done.

Contents

List of Figures

Introduction

Good intentions, idyllic wishes, and flawed policies do not improve people's lives.

Like so many other Americans, I am a product of people who came to this country in search of a better life. Three of my grandparents were of Anglo-Saxon and one was of German descent. My Anglo-Saxon ancestors came to America in the seventeenth and eighteenth centuries, and my German ancestors in the nineteenth century. And like so many other Americans, life improved for each generation of my ancestors throughout our country's history. Sadly, this has not been the case for the current generation, as our nation no longer exhibits the vitality and the promise that it did in prior decades.

Many American children live with one parent and grow up in poverty. Many receive a poor education. Many families cannot access or afford good healthcare. When adjusted for inflation, most American incomes have stagnated for twenty-seven years. We have unprecedented levels of debt. Unknown numbers of criminals, terrorists, and unvaccinated people enter the country illegally each year. Immigrant assimilation is no longer a priority, and a common language and culture no longer unify us. Inequality increases. Social mobility declines. Polarizing politics, laws, policies, news, and speech divide us. Dysfunctional federal and state governments fail us.

If these challenges were not enough, we degrade our ecosystems and spew billions of tons of climate-altering carbon dioxide into the atmosphere each year. Radical Islam and terrorists threaten us everywhere. China and Russia expand their geographic influence and footprint. The maniacal, repressive regimes of Iran and North Korea oppress their people and threaten the rest of us. Why are our challenges mounting, and why are we no longer ascending?

In 1978, at age nineteen, I participated in an economic development field study of Guatemala, Costa Rica, Honduras, and Columbia. At one of our stops, we visited a family in a one-room home in Columbia. The home had a dirt floor, it was fly infested, and the parents and seven children slept on mats. A year later, I participated in an agricultural field study of Western Europe, Eastern Europe, and the former Soviet Union. The contrasts between life in Upstate New York and many of these countries shocked me and started me pondering why some populations prosper and others merely subsist.

Although there are many causes of individual and national prosperity, I recognized at an early age that the overarching one is culture.

> **Culture** is human software that orchestrates activity. It is the perspectives, practices, and taboos that parents, teachers, and others transmit to us, and the art, heroes, and achievements that groups celebrate to reinforce the transmission.

International economic and cultural differences were not the only ones that I experienced during my college years. Soon after starting, I ran headlong into our country's great cultural divide. Raised in rural America, I was given a strong Protestant faith and many accompanying perspectives and practices. In college, I found that most professors had little use for them. Wanting to do well in school, I gave the professors the secular perspectives they wanted and kept the faith-based ones to myself.

After completing my undergraduate education in 1980, I again traveled behind the Iron Curtain, this time to Poland to teach English composition to scientists. I chose Poland because of the great ferment in the country and its many cultural contrasts to the United States. Most adults had full-time jobs and had to queue up for fifteen to twenty hours a week just to purchase their food and household supplies. They lived in small apartments and remained poor despite what they did. Their government prohibited travel to Western countries and censored their communications, news, books, and periodicals.

Just before my arrival, Karol Wojtyła, the charismatic cardinal from Cracow, became Pope John Paul II. His election gave the Poles tremendous confidence. While I was there, most Poles went on strike and gathered in the churches to protest their living standards and lack of freedom. All my students were members of Solidarity, the first independent labor union in a Soviet-bloc country. President Reagan and Margaret Thatcher encouraged and supported the Poles' strikes and protests. Lech Wałesa, Pope John Paul II, and Cardinal Wyszyński, the Roman Catholic Primate of Poland, orchestrated them.

Cosmos and *Dragons of Eden* by Carl Sagan were two of the several books that I had brought with me. They described the evolution of the universe and human intelligence. I read and reflected upon these books and on all that I had learned in the prior three years. The better acquainted I became with science's explanation of the universe and life, the more I realized that my childhood faith rested on incredulous, unsubstantiated stories. My faith conveniently dismissed important scientific perspectives that better explained the origin and workings of the universe and life.

Awestruck with the cosmos and science and skeptical of my religious tenets, I came to favor scientific thought over the faith-based tenets and begrudgingly underwent the religious-to-secular transformation that millions of other people have undergone.

By age twenty-six, I had traveled to forty-five states and twenty-six countries. I had lived in two states and two countries and completed my BS and MS degrees, and courses for a PhD. Plus, I had read some two hundred of the world's most thought-provoking books. I had detected the primary question that has preoccupied me for years, confronted our cultural divide, and embraced evidence-based knowledge.

Through my exposure to various cultures and thoughts, I encountered many conflicting perspectives and practices. As someone who is inquisitive, is contemplative, and values intellectual consistency, the conflicts did not sit well with me. They forced me to evaluate many of my childhood paradigms and grapple with many questions, such as: How did the universe and life arise? What are the implications of science's narratives?

Authoritarianism or democracy, nationalism or federalism, capital-ism or socialism—what works best? What enables large middle classes to emerge and flourish? What fueled the extraordinary rise of the English Commonwealth countries, the United States, Western Europe, Japan, South Korea, Taiwan, Hong Kong, and Singapore? What is universal to human life, and what is unique to a group, locale, or country? How do we prevent recessions, depressions, and inflation?

Why did our country's founders so distrust concentrations of power? Why are conservatives sometimes right and liberals sometimes right? Why are the results of many public policies antithetical to their supporters' intentions? Why do people make so many decisions that inflict future suffering upon themselves and others?

Despite my shattered paradigms and many questions, I functioned reasonably well, drawing upon the values and habits of my youth. How-ever, when my wife placed our son in my arms, I experienced a bit of a crisis. He came with no instruction book. What was I going to teach him? Given the perspectives and knowledge gained over the last five hundred years, what does a child need to learn? What fosters our health, effectiveness, longevity, civility, and happiness? How do we adapt our lifestyles to live responsibly and do no harm?

These questions and our great faith versus science, right versus left cultural divide have haunted me for years. The divide itself separates families, communities, and the citizens of our country. It diminishes our fitness, effectiveness, social cohesiveness, and children's futures. Having spent time on both sides of it, I have friends who have a faith and ones who have no faith.

The great irony of the cultural divide is that each side has some-thing the other lacks. People of faith maintain an empowering culture, and people of science build an empowering knowledge base. People of faith understand that doing the right thing yields positive effects, and the people of science understand that life is what we make of it.

For many years, I raised my family, built three businesses, and sat on numerous community, state, and national boards. I read hundreds of books, traveled to many more states and countries, attended educational programs, ran for Congress, and pondered my earlier questions and the positions and insights of faith communities, scientists, conservatives, and progressives.

Eventually, I realized that most of us lack the interest and maturity to comprehend the evolution of the universe and life and their implications when we're in high school, and unless we study the physical and biological sciences in college, we generally never fully grasp them. This is unfortunate, because if we take the time to understand evolution, and integrate its perspectives into our thinking, we can improve our effectiveness and lives immeasurably.

The *Flourish* Series is about the perspectives and practices, or the culture, that cause a population to thrive. This book, the first of the series, discusses how America lost its way, how the average American is doing relative to the average Singaporean and Swiss citizen, and eight perspectives—Truth, Causality, Scale, Evolution, Fitness, Human Nature, Periodic Disaster, and Eco-Dependency—that come from evolution and science. The second book in this series, *Winning Practices of a Free, Fit, and Prosperous People*, describes thrity-six individual, family, education, enterprise, and government practices that further a population's fitness and well-being.

> **Winning Perspectives** are accurate perceptions of reality and conditions of existence. Substantial evidence exists for them.

> **Winning Practices** are actions that positively affect individuals, groups, and/or the environment in the short and long term.

The better we understand the Winning Perspectives, the easier it is to identify Winning Practices. The more we employ Winning Practices, the more we flourish.

Our country is at a critical crossroads. In more credibly explaining our context, origin, and nature, scientists undermined the Judeo-Christian worldview and many of its tenets. In changing how we elect U.S. Senators in 1913 and reinterpreting the "general welfare" clause of the Constitution, progressives broke critical restraints. Reacting to their historic mistreatment, separation, and ongoing discrimination, many African Americans embrace an oppressor-oppressed, anti-Caucasian counterculture. Lacking English proficiency and legal status, many Hispanics do not assimilate.

The Constitution, rule of law, limited federal government, a strong defense, free enterprise, legal immigration, intact families, charter schools, work, and economic ascendance characterize the interests of the right-leaning coalition, while unionization, public education and healthcare, improved opportunities for women and minorities, the redistribution of wealth, larger government and more regulation, the admission of people of color into the country, the environment, and the advancement of social justice characterize the left-leaning coalition's interests. Lacking unifying leadership and culture, we fight among ourselves, lurch left, then right, and stagnate. The prevalence of Winning Perspectives and Practices decreases, and the prevalence of losing perspectives and practices increases in our population.

The path forward is relatively clear to many people, but ignorance, opposing ideologies, and vested interests hinder us. Our past success, accumulated wealth, and tremendous capacity to borrow enable us to ignore our problems and to be foolish for a long time. The Winning Perspectives and Practices in the *Flourish* Series serve everyone's interests. They are a synthesis of many of the world's most empowering perspectives and practices. Health, prosperity, long life, and greatly diminished heartache await those who understand, employ, perpetuate, and improve them.

CHAPTER 1

Losing Our Way

We thought we were different . . . more able, prosperous, and blessed.
And we were more of these things, as we were more honest, hardworking, and
responsible, as we took marriage, parenting, and education more seriously,
and as we were more community and country minded.

One of the most telling indications that our country is losing its way
is the relative change in American and Chinese living standards between
1990 and 2015. In 1990, American living standards were seventy-five
times greater than Chinese living standards. In 2015, they were seven
times higher.[1]

Chinese living standards have improved steadily while our living
standards have stagnated. Figure 1 shows real and hypothetical growing
U.S. household incomes between 1990 and 2015. Adjusted for inflation,
our real median income has been flat for a generation. If it had increased
3 percent a year during this period, more of a historical norm, it would
be $107,000 rather than $54,000!

Figure 1: Median Household Income 1990-2015
Actual vs Hypothetical Growing at 3% Per Year

United States Census Bureau, Data, Income Data Tables, Table H-8 Median Household Income by State, https://www.census.gov/data/tables/time-series/demo/income-poverty/historical-income-households.html

Amazingly, the Chinese economy became almost as large as the U.S. economy in 2016. If the two economies continue to grow at their current relative rates, then the Chinese economy will be two times larger than ours in twelve years and four times larger in twenty-four years.

Rising living standards in China are a great thing, but the combination of Chinese ascendancy and American decline is not good for Western values and populations. The Chinese have their own interests and values, many of which compete with ours. As China rises and America declines, China will reshape the international order to reflect their interests and values. China will encourage one-party rule around the world rather than constitutional democracies and the rule of law. It will encourage state prerogatives over individual rights. It will seize control of South Pacific shipping lanes and make the terms of trade more favorable for China and less favorable to other countries. China's currency, the renminbi, may even replace the dollar as the reserve currency of the world, decreasing American living standards an additional 10 to 20 percent.

Rising Chinese living standards and stagnant American living standards are not our only challenges. Radical Islam and Islamic population growth are also serious problems. While our leaders hesitate to acknowledge it, the Western and Islamic cultures collide. Where we value democratic and secular government, individual rights, and male and female parity, most Islamic leaders value authoritarian and religious rule, religious orthodoxy, and male dominance.

While we may find it incomprehensible that large numbers of Muslims hate us, the fact is that many do. Our promiscuous lifestyles, dysfunctional families, alcohol and drug abuse, and high crime rates are unappealing to them. Our freedoms, gender equality, and tolerance undermine their patterns of life. Our priorities, might, and actions thwart their leaders' aspirations.

To these three serious challenges, I would add seven more: (1) a failure to develop and educate many children, (2) a failure to integrate many African Americans, Hispanics, and Muslims in our country, (3) our government's dysfunction and propensity to live beyond its means, (4) our emissions of large quantities of greenhouse gases, (5) the degradation of ecosystems and ground water, (6) the eradication of many species, and (7) the tendency for Winning Perspectives and Practices to decrease in prevalence within our culture and losing perspectives and practices to increase.

While each of these challenges is discussed in more detail later in this and the next book, this chapter focuses on our declining vitality and the causes of the decreasing prevalence of Winning Perspectives and Practices within our country.

Inclusion Failures

Our ancestors provided us with a stunning start. Their pragmatism, ideals, and newly minted government were extraordinary. Their courage, hard work, sacrifice, and perseverance were legendary. The problem with our start was that our ancestors took our country from the Native Americans, and enslaved Africans. The institution of slavery and eradication of most Native Americans were travesties. While we have acknowledged the horrific treatment of Native Americans and ended slavery, we have yet to integrate many Native and African Americans into our communities.

Our destruction of the Native American culture was genocide and a lost opportunity. Had we treated Native Americans more honorably and shared more of the continent with them, we might have acquired their reverence for the environment. We might emit less carbon and fewer pollutants, be healthier, and have a brighter future.

Our inclusion failures were not only at the start, though. They have occurred in every decade since. Segregation, discrimination, and education dysfunction have created mistrust, animosity, and depravity within minority communities. They have created a destructive subculture, unsafe neighborhoods, broken families, widespread alcohol and drug addiction, and millions of poorly parented children.

Worldwide, majorities naturally discriminate against minorities. People favor those most like them. This behavior is instinctual. "Birds of a feather flock together" and "You can tell a zebra by its stripes" are adages indicative of this tendency. And while this instinct may have served hunter-gatherers well, it serves us poorly. A people composed of different races, ethnicities, and creeds must overcome discriminatory behavior with education, training, and legal recourse.

The lack of a clean start and our integration failures divide us. They diminish minority actualization and contribution. They increase our social welfare burdens and decrease our living standards. They reduce the prevalence of Winning Practices within our culture, diminish our social cohesion, and reduce our ability to overcome challenges.

The Change in the Election of U.S. Senators

> The powers delegated by the proposed Constitution to the federal government are few and defined. Those which are to remain in the State governments are numerous and indefinite.[2]
>
> —James Madison

Our founders limited the scope of the federal government in the Constitution, and they enforced this limited scope with the way Senators were elected. We broke the enforcement mechanism when we passed the Seventeenth Amendment in 1913. Before the amendment, state legislatures chose the U.S. Senators. After it, the people of each state elected the senators. Where state legislator–selected senators limited federal power, citizen-selected ones expand it.

Except for a ten-year period around the Civil War, our federal government's expenditures as a percent of gross national product (GNP) were less than 4 percent for the first 125 years of our nation's history. As figure 2 illustrates, the passage of the Seventeenth Amendment changed this. Over the subsequent hundred years, federal expenditures as a percent of GNP grew more than nine-fold from 2.5 percent to 21 percent. Add state and local expenditures to this, and government spending comprises 35 percent of GNP.

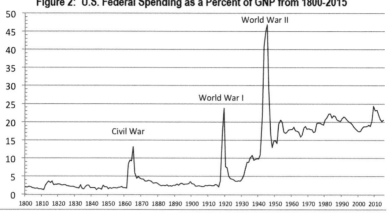

Figure 2: U.S. Federal Spending as a Percent of GNP from 1800-2015

Measuring Worth, Data Sets, US Nominal GDP, https://www.measuringworth.com/
Government Spending, Download Spending Data,
Multiyear Download of US Government Spending 1800–2015
http://www.usgovernmentspending.com/download_multi_year_1792_2015USb_17s2li001mcn_F0f

Since 1913, our federal government has expanded its powers significantly and become a wasteful, inefficient, and corrupt colossus. It regulates every aspect of our life, burdening its citizens and stifling the economy. The stories of the state governments are more mixed. States such as New York, Illinois, and California have created larger governments, stifling their residents' living standards, while states like Florida, Indiana, South Carolina, and Texas have maintained smaller governments, enabling their residents' living standards to improve steadily.

Ending the state legislature check on the federal government was one of our greatest mistakes, as now special interests buy our elected representatives with campaign contributions, and our elected representatives buy our votes with legislative and public spending favors. Too much government burdens a country, just as too much overhead and debt burden families and companies. You only need to compare the great gains that people made and continue to make throughout the world when their government spending is in the 5 to 15 percent of GNP range to the small increases that occur when this ratio exceeds 20 percent. The histories of Canada, the United States, Western Europe, and Japan all demonstrate this reality.

Presidential Constitutional Failings

Whether we liked presidents Theodore Roosevelt, Wilson, Franklin Roosevelt, Truman, Johnson, Nixon, Bush 41, Clinton, Bush 43, and Obama and their policies, their flagrant failures to defend the Constitution and their abuses of power should trouble us.

World history is one long chronology of governments abusing their citizens. Only with the signing of the Magna Carta by King John in 1215, the signing of the Petition of Right by King Charles I in 1628, and the passage of the Bill of Rights in 1689 did English-speaking people have freedom from the arbitrary and oppressive yoke of their rulers. Only with the adoption of the Articles of Confederation in 1781, the Constitution of the United States of America in 1788, and the first ten amendments known as the Bill of Rights in 1791 did our ancestors free us of this yoke.

The Constitution of the United States is one of the most important documents ever written. Hundreds of millions of Americans as well as other people around the world have had much better lives because of it. If you have not read it, I highly recommend that you do so. It is ingenious, understandable, and only about twenty-five pages.

The framers of our government knew the Constitution and its specified institutions, procedures, and requirements were imperfect and that the country's needs would change over time. Thus, they included a provision to amend the Constitution where two-thirds of Congress or two-thirds of the states could request an amendment, and three-quarters of the state legislatures must ratify it. The procedure gives us time to thoroughly consider a change and requires widespread support. Amending the Constitution is difficult, perhaps too difficult, as it has only been amended twenty-seven times in 220 years.

From 1777 to 1900, Americans appreciated their Constitution—its separation of power, checks on power, and specified institutions, procedures, and requirements. Most of the government leaders took their oaths of office seriously, preserving and defending the Constitution. Unfortunately, this changed with the election of Theodore Roosevelt and has continued unabated ever since.

This flagrant failure to uphold and defend the document that defines the separation of power, checks on power, governing processes, and our rights jeopardizes our freedoms. Common presidential misuse of the government to reward supporters and punish opponents delegitimizes the government and polarizes us. Brion McClanahan catalogues and explains many presidential failings and abuses of power in his book *9 Presidents Who Screwed Up America*. Some of these presidential failings and abuses of power appear in figure 3.

What are some of the ways that twentieth- and twenty-first-century presidents have failed to preserve, protect, and defend the Constitution? Starting with Theodore Roosevelt and contrary to the separation of the legislative, executive, and judicial functions in the Constitution, numerous presidents have used the executive office, presidential favors, and executive orders to push legislative agendas. Teddy Roosevelt's Square Deal, seizure of 230 million acres of land, and 1,081 executive orders; Woodrow Wilson's New Freedom legislation and 1,803 executive orders; and Franklin Roosevelt's New Deal and 3,734 executive orders, one of which confiscated much of the gold in the country, all are examples of presidential violations of the Constitution. Lyndon Johnson's Great Society legislation and 325 executive orders and George W. Bush's 291 executive orders, many of which ignored fundamental American rights, are other serious presidential violations of the Constitution.[3]

Several presidents have supported the federal government's assumption of powers that "the people" never granted to it. Franklin Roosevelt used the influence of the presidency to enact Food Stamps, Welfare, and Social Security; Lyndon Johnson to involve the federal government in education, healthcare, the arts, and public broadcasting; and Barack Obama to control the healthcare system.

Figure 3: Presidential Constitutional Failings

THEODORE ROOSEVELT

The Food and Drug and the Meat Inspection Acts of 1906

Proclamations to Seize 230 Million Acres of Land

The Use of the Military in the Panama Revolution

WOODROW WILSON

The Federal Reserve Act of 1913

Clayton Trust Act of 1914

Federal Trade Commission Act of 1914

The Federal Loan Administration of 1916

Selective Service Act of 1917

War Industries Board, War Labor Board, Federal Fuel Administration

The Sedition Act of 1918

The Nationalization of Radio and Committee of Public Information Act

Use of the Military in Several Countries

FRANKLIN ROOSEVELT

Agricultural Adjustment Act and National Industrial Recovery Acts of 1933

Civilian Works Administration and Civilian Conservation Corps

Executive Order Confiscating Gold in 1933

The National Housing Act of 1934

The Labor Relations Board and Export Boards

Banking Act of 1935

Social Security Act of 1935

The Supreme Court Packing Threat in 1937

HARRY TRUMAN

The Seizure of Numerous Private Businesses

The Continuation of Price Controls after the War

The Appropriation of Large Sums for the Marshall Plan and Cold War

The Use of the United States Military as Agent of the United Nations

LYNDON JOHNSON

Clean Air and Endangered Species Preservation Acts of 1963 and 1966

Economic Opportunities and Food Stamp Acts of 1964

The Elementary and Secondary Education Act of 1965

Higher Education and Appalachian Region Development Acts of 1965

The Social Security Act of 1965, adding Medicare and Medicaid

Housing and Urban Development Act of 1965

Water Quality Act and Solid Waste Disposal Acts of 1965

The National Foundation of the Arts and Humanities Act of 1965

The Public Broadcasting Act of 1967

The Bilingual Education Act of 1968

The Escalation of the War in Vietnam without a Declaration of War

RICHARD NIXON

National Environmental Policy Act of 1969

Clean Air Act of 1970

Department of Interior's Creation of 642 National Parks

Occupational Safety and Health Act of 1970

Enforcement of School Busing

Established Racial Goals and Timetables

Education Amendments of 1972 and Title IX

Cancelation of the Bretton Woods Agreement

Myth of Executive Privilege and the Watergate Cover-Up

GEORGE W. BUSH

USA Patriot Act of 2001

Invasion of Iraq without a Congressional Declaration of War

No Child Left Behind Act of 2001

Medicare Act of 2003

Housing and Economic Recovery Act of 2008

Executive Orders Violating Basic American Rights

BARACK OBAMA

Appointments to Oversee Agencies without Congressional Consent

Granted Work Waivers to Welfare Recipients

Stripped the Creditors of GM and Chrysler of Their Money

Moratorium on Offshore Drilling

Patient Protection and Affordable Care Act of 2010

Delayed the ACA Unlawfully 28 Times

Used the IRS against Conservative Groups

Unlawful Appointments to the National Labor Relations Board

Illegal Appointments to the Consumer Protection Board

Circumvented the Freedom of Information Act

Ordered to Close a Company Plant and Fire Nonunion Workers

Refused to Prosecute Violators of Drug Laws

Encouraged Violations of the Immigration and Naturalization Laws

Use of the Military in Libya and Syria without Declarations of War

Some presidents have created executive agencies with the ability to create regulations, execute them, and adjudicate them. Woodrow Wilson did this with the Federal Trade Commission. Richard Nixon did this with the Occupational Safety and Health Administration and Environmental Protection Agency.

Some presidents have treated various groups more favorably or unfavorably than other ones. Woodrow Wilson exempted agricultural organizations and labor unions from antitrust laws with the Clayton Antitrust Act of 1914, and Barack Obama's Internal Revenue Agency discriminated against conservative groups.

Several recent presidents also have violated their oaths to preserve, protect, and defend the Constitution with their selective enforcement of federal laws. Barack Obama, one of the most unlawful presidents in our country's history, made appointments to oversee the executive departments, National Labor Relations Board, and federal courts, all without congressional consent. He unlawfully delayed the implementation of the Affordable Healthcare Act twenty-eight times. He did not enforce many drug laws and released thousands of federal prisoners. Worst of all, he not only failed to enforce the immigration and naturalization laws but encouraged foreigners to violate them by (a) restricting the 287(g) program that permits police officers to apprehend illegal immigrants who are stopped for other crimes, (b) ignoring the thirty-one sanctuary cities that protect illegal immigrants, and (c) curtailing funding for a program designed to find visitors who overstay their visas.[4]

The Constitution of the United States of America gives Congress the power to declare war and the president the power to make treaties. Theodore Roosevelt used the military in the Panama Revolution without a declaration of war from Congress. Woodrow Wilson used the military in several Latin American countries and Russia. Lyndon Johnson did this in Vietnam, Ronald Reagan in Grenada, and Barack Obama in Libya and Syria. Harry Truman used the U.S. military as an agent of the United Nations, and Bill Clinton used it forty times around the world.[5] Historian Brion McClanahan writes:

The slew of executive legislative initiatives since the 1930s has forced Americans to believe that American government is executive government, regardless of political party. We feel confident in our guy in office and think little of the potential ramifications should our guy be out of office and the other guy take his place. Republicans who insist on impeaching Obama for his unconstitutional acts are the same who defended George W. Bush and his unconstitutional acts, and vice versa. Inconsistency and excessive partisanship—something George Washington warned against in his Farewell Address—have inflicted terrible damage on the American experiment in republican self-government.[6]

This is not to suggest that we should not deal with crises quickly, end discrimination, look out for the poor, assist some seniors, preserve habitats, curb pollution, and defend ourselves. Approaches consistent with the Constitution exist to do all these things, and I describe many of them in *Winning Practices of a Free, Fit, and Prosperous People.*

People wonder why our federal government is so expensive, intrusive in our lives, partisan, and dysfunctional. While there are many reasons, certainly our failure to hold our presidents accountable to the Constitution is a primary one. For more than half of the presidents in the twentieth and twenty-first centuries to take an oath to uphold the Constitution and then to repeatedly violate it does not bode well for our country. For Congress not to impeach these presidents is irresponsible. For the press not to expose these presidents' unconstitutional acts is unconscionable.

Whether we are aware of it or not, our freedom, living standards, and well-being depend upon our Constitution and the rule of law—and on people's respect for and adherence to them. When government leaders violate our Constitution and our laws, we must impeach them. When they ignore the unconstitutional and unlawful actions of our presidents, we must not re-elect them. When journalists ignore these leaders' unconstitutional and unlawful actions, we must boycott their organizations. If we impeached a couple of presidents, did not re-elect a few more representatives, and reduced our patronage of the most irresponsible news organizations, we would curtail these inattentive and politically based omissions. Failure to do these things places everything we hold dear in jeopardy. As James Madison wrote:

> There are more instances of the abridgment of the freedom of the people by gradual and silent encroachments of those in power than by violent and sudden usurpations.[7]

Supreme Court Constitutional Failings

Constitutional decoupling involves the periodic failure of the U.S. Supreme Court to strike down unconstitutional legislation and executive actions. It results from presidential appointments of justices who are more interested in advancing political agendas than upholding the Constitution. It enables Congress to usurp many state powers, and the Executive branch to usurp judicial and legislative powers.

James Madison was very clear on the limited, specified powers of the federal government and the intended interpretation of the "general welfare" clause:

> With respect to the words "general welfare," I have always regarded them as qualified by the detail of powers connected with them. To take them in a literal and unlimited sense would be a metamorphosis of the Constitution into a character which there is a host of proofs was not contemplated by its creators.[8]

Who would have foreseen that a few well-placed progressives could transform our federal government with a reinterpretation of these two words? It took over a century, a national crisis, an activist president, and a cohort of liberal judges, but this did finally happen during the Franklin Delano Roosevelt presidency. Like water breaching a dike, once the "general welfare" clause was reinterpreted, the powers of the federal government have grown unceasingly. Since the 1960s, the Legislative branch commonly creates unconstitutional laws, the Executive branch acts unconstitutionally, and the Supreme Court sits passively by.

Congress legislates, taxes, and spends in ways that favor some groups over others. The federal and state governments interfere with private contracts and redistribute wealth. Congress passes poorly defined laws, and regulatory agencies fill in the details. The Executive branch interprets laws and judges their validity. Federal and state governments seize private property for economic gain. Government and institutions use racial preferences. Detail regarding some of these Supreme Court constitutional failings can be found in Appendix B.

Abiding by the Constitution and our laws is in everyone's long-term interests. If something needs doing that the Constitution does not allow, state legislatures and federal government representatives can amend the Constitution and change the laws. Only the states and representatives of the people are authorized under the Constitution to expand the power of the federal government. Individual presidents and five justices should not be doing this.

Special Interest Government

With the state legislature check on the growth of the federal government eliminated in 1913 and other constitutional checks destroyed by the Supreme Court in the 1930s and 1940s, federal legislation and expenditures, and special interests protective of them, grow and grow. To see this, think of the federal government's importance to Social Security, Medicaid, Welfare, and Food Stamp recipients, as well as public sector contractors, unions, and employees.

Crony capitalism is a form of special interest government that occurs when business leaders make large campaign contributions to candidates who later do favors for them. The favors take the form of permitting oligopolistic market concentrations, supporting legislation that is advantageous to contributors, and/or awarding government contracts and grants to contributors' businesses. While some of these favors are advantageous to everyone, most of them benefit the contributors and harm taxpayers and consumers.

Unionization is another form of special interest government that occurs when union leaders make large campaign contributions to candidates to incentivize them to pass legislation that increases unions' abilities to extract money and benefits from taxpayers and employers. While this exchange seems harmless to many, the favors decrease the competitiveness of enterprises and increase the cost of public and private products and services.

When people allow their central government to become large, it responds to special interests more than to citizen interests. Special interests buy elected officials, and elected officials buy people's votes with reckless borrowing, taxing, and spending, exchanges that diminish our living standards and future.

Less Faith-Community Relevance

As science exposes more of the cause-and-effect relationships of the universe, life, and related processes, it inadvertently decreases the credibility of religions. Religious teachings, rewards, and penalties—like an eternal afterlife in heaven or hell—lose sway over progressives first, moderates second, and eventually many conservatives. When religious institutions lose progressives, they slow their adaptation. They lose the ability to keep their perspectives, practices, heroes, and art forms relevant to new generations, and they lose the opportunity to teach large portions of the population to act in an honest, responsible, civil, and considerate manner.

We see the decline of faith communities in the change in Christian church attendance in the last fifty years. Where over 60 percent of the U.S. population regularly attended services in 1960, less than 20 percent of the population regularly attended services in 2005.[9] The reduced influence of a dominant institution across 40 percent of the U.S. population coincides with the decline of honesty and civility in our culture.

Less Integrity, Responsibility, and Civility

As faith communities emphasizing responsible conduct and service lose relevance, one would think that people would exhibit less of these characteristics, especially if other institutions did not teach and positively reinforce these behaviors. And this is exactly what has happened. Spouses have become less committed to each other. Parents have become less respectful of principals, teachers, and coaches. Children have become less respectful of parents, teachers, and police. Employers and employees have become less conscientious about their responsibilities to one another and less attentive to what is best for others.

Consider that 25 percent of our population ages eighteen and older now engage regularly in heavy drinking.[10] Roughly 15 percent of Americans ages twelve and older use illicit drugs each year, and almost 50 percent use them sometime in their lifetimes.[11] Over 40 percent of Americans ages 18-59 had a sexually transmitted disease (STD) in the last five years.[12] Sixty-six percent of all traffic fatalities are caused by aggressive driving.[13] The U.S. ranking on the World Corruption Perception Index has dropped to 17th place in the last ten years.[14] The U.S. ranks 35th among 120 countries in incidents of crime. Iran, Saudi Arabia, Israel, Azerbaijan, Turkey, Ethiopia, India, and Russia all report lower incidents of crime than the U.S.[15] The prevalence of heavy drinking, illicit drug use, STDs, preventable traffic fatalities, corruption, and crime are not characteristic of an ascending population.

Promiscuity and the Decline of Marriage

Before the 1950s, most men and women married at a relatively young age, remained married for life, and provided a stable home environment for their children. Since the 1950s, marriage rates have fallen by two-thirds, and separation and divorce rates have increased three times.[16] Incidents of promiscuity, cohabitation, and divorce have increased precipitously with the declining influence of religion, the development of highly reliable forms of birth control, the changing roles of women, and the implementation of generous Welfare programs. Now, half of all marriages fail, and more than half of all children grow up in a single-parent household and nontraditional family.

These new patterns of life have a greater impact on non-college graduates than on those who finish college. Robert Putnam, professor of public policy at Harvard University, writes:

> In the college-educated, upper third of American society, a "neo-traditional" marriage pattern has emerged. It mirrors the 1950s family in many respects, except that both partners now typically work outside of the home, they delay marriage and childbearing until their careers are under way, and they divide domestic duties more evenly. . . .

> In the high-school-educated, lower third of the population, by contrast, a new, more kaleidoscopic pattern began to emerge in which childbearing became increasingly disconnected from marriage, and sexual partnerships became less durable.[17]

The adverse effects of these new patterns of life on the economically challenged lower third of our population should concern all of us, as we cannot flourish for long as a people when one-third of our children grow up in dysfunctional families, neighborhoods, and schools.

Poorly Parented Children

While some parents who maintain healthy lifelong marriages do a poor job of parenting children, and some parents who separate and/or have multiple mates do a good job, generally the former group of parents do a better job. Parents of traditional families have greater commitments to each other and their children. They provide their children more parental time, resources, and stability; a healthier balance of nurture, discipline, and expectation; and greater educational and mentoring opportunities.

Professor Putnam indicates that in the 1960s, 6 percent of children in the U.S. lived in nontraditional families, but today more than half of all children do. He also indicates that children with parents in the lowest educational quartile are roughly two times more likely to live with one parent during their childhood than those with parents in the highest quartile.[18] And while some nontraditional parents do a fantastic job raising their children, the research indicates that most do not do well. Professor Putnam writes:

> Children who grow up without their biological father perform worse on standardized tests, earn lower grades, and stay in school for fewer years, regardless of race and class. They are also more likely to demonstrate behavioral problems such as shyness, aggression, and psychological problems such as increased anxiety and depression. Children who spend part of their childhood in a single-mother home are also more likely to have sex earlier and to become young, single parents, re-creating the cycle.

> Children in divorced or remarried families face distinctive challenges, partly because their families' limited resources must be spread across more than one household, and partly because their parents' lingering grievances, and physical and emotional distance from one another, hamper effective communication and coordination. Multi-partner fertility is associated with less parental involvement, less extended kin involvement, and more friction, jealousy, and competition, especially when there are children from different partnerships living in the same household.[19]

Unionization of Education

In the 1960s, the Democratic Party and union leaders saw an opportunity to increase their power and following by unionizing the public sector. Undoubtedly, public employee compensation was low in some areas, and some school boards and superintendents were undesirable employers. Yet, some fifty years later, it is painfully clear that the ill effects of this change outweigh the benefits.

Primary and secondary education have become less effective and costlier throughout the country. Proportionally fewer children develop basic math, reading, writing, and speaking skills. Proportionally fewer children acquire winning perspectives, possess empowering habits, and employ as many winning practices. Proportionally fewer children are well equipped to parent children, have productive careers, and become responsible citizens. Some fifty years later, we spend proportionally more on education and obtain poorer results.

Union work rules, seniority-based compensation, and tenure hinder the employment of the ablest administrators and teachers. They prevent administrators from adjusting teachers' compensation in accordance with their performance. They make it difficult for administrators to terminate poor-performing employees, and they create unaffordable pension liabilities.

Schools matter! They make us individually and collectively fit or weak. We devote thirteen to seventeen years of our lives to them. They affect our lives tremendously, and they must perform at a high level.

Liberalization of Education

Union work rules, seniority-based compensation, and tenure politicize education. They cause administrators and teachers to support the candidates for public office who support unions. They increase the number of administrators and teachers who register as Democrats and donate to the Democratic Party, and they decrease the number who register and give to the competing parties. They fill public education with administrators and teachers who look unfavorably on many of the Winning Practices that enable us to flourish.

Now, disproportionate numbers of public educators dislike the limited, decentralized federal government upon which our freedoms and living standards depend. They dislike the competition and meritocracy that drive free enterprise and free markets, and they dislike the educational rigor that yielded good results for generations.

Most public schools no longer group students by their ability. Most are hesitant to discipline children and uphold basic behavioral and academic standards. Many public schools no longer give children credit for doing homework, and some forbid teachers from assigning it. Many public schools give students multiple opportunities to retake the tests, sabotaging the opportunity to instill the habit of preparation in students.

Liberalized public schools dumb down curriculum, inflate grades, and advance many students who fail to master the material. They promote cultural relativism, nonjudgmentalism, and multiculturalism, concepts that I discuss later in this chapter. They do not give children a sense of the practices that enable us to prosper, like a constitutional, limited, representative federal government; free enterprise; and free markets. Not having a healthy mix of conservatives, moderates, and progressives teaching children in public schools contributes mightily to our country's poorer educational, social, and economic outcomes.

Social Justice Missteps

Given the genocide, slavery, discrimination, segregation, and limitations on women in our history, many of our greatest heroes were advocates of social justice. People like Horace Mann, Frederick Douglass, Harriet Beecher Stowe, Booker T. Washington, Elizabeth Cady Stanton, Susan B. Anthony, John Steinbeck, Jackie Robinson, Martin Luther King Jr., and Betty Friedan worked tirelessly to break social barriers and improve the lives of women and minorities. These heroes, good-hearted souls, all rejected hatred, retribution, and violence in their push for change. Their pursuit of social justice was clearly advantageous. It was good for the victims of injustice and the larger population.

And herein lies an important distinction. The pursuit of social justice is advantageous and laudable when it makes us more conscious of injustice, breaks senseless barriers, advances opportunity, and improves our attitudes, norms, and laws. It is advantageous and laudable when it empowers individuals, increases personal responsibility, advances education and work opportunities, and furthers civility, social cohesion, and prosperity. On the other hand, the pursuit of social justice is ignoble and counterproductive when it employs deception, lawlessness, and violence; favors some people over others; undermines and excuses personal responsibility; seeks equal outcomes; and furthers animosity and dependence.

Safe neighborhoods, school choice, remedial educational opportunities, antidiscrimination laws, and work opportunities are advantageous to the victims of social injustice and the larger population. Tolerance of crime and discrimination; free housing, food, and education; encouragement of illegal immigration; lower admission standards; excusing disruptive behavior; irresponsible borrowing, taxing, and spending; and permissive monetary policy are disadvantageous to victims and the larger population.

While many politicians fan social justice concerns to garner political support, we avoided supporting the counterproductive approaches until the presidencies of Franklin Roosevelt, Harry Truman, Lyndon Johnson, Richard Nixon, and Barack Obama. We avoided disadvantageous responses for more than 150 years, but as our regard for the Constitution waned, opportunistic leaders employed irresponsible approaches, sowing the seeds of discord, polarization, and decline.

Cultural Relativism, Nonjudgmentalism, and Multiculturalism

Cultural relativism is the belief that truth exists in relation to culture, society, and historical context. Nonjudgmentalism is the idea that we should not judge others because they are a product of their culture and context. Multiculturalism is the idea that all cultures are equally meritorious. The appeal of cultural relativism, nonjudgmentalism, and multiculturalism is that there is an element of truth to them, they further tolerance, and they make people feel good about themselves.

The problem with cultural relativism, nonjudgmentalism, and multiculturalism is that they are not completely true. Some perspectives and practices further people's well-being better than others. We must be able to judge the desirability of perspectives and practices, and what works "best" is not always relative; sometimes it is universal.

Cultural relativism, nonjudgmentalism, and multiculturalism discourage the discrimination between winning and losing perspectives and practices, opening people up to a whole array of counterproductive ones. Their absurdity becomes more apparent in the extreme, as in determining the relative desirability of the Swiss and Haitian cultures and Singaporean and North Korean cultures. Yale professor and *New York Times* columnist David Brooks writes of this cultural challenge in his column "The Cost of Relativism":

> We now have multiple generations of people caught in recurring feedback loops of economic stress and family breakdown. . . . It's not only money and better policy that are missing in these circles; it's norms. . . . These norms weren't destroyed because of people with bad values. They were destroyed by a plague of nonjudgmentalism, which refused to assert that one way of behaving was better than another.[20]

With the liberalization of education, cultural relativism, nonjudgmentalism, and multiculturalism became actively promoted in our public schools and universities. Extreme tolerance and the idea that all cultures are equally desirable supplanted a mature discrimination between winning and losing perspectives and practices, as well as the idea that the American culture had something important to offer immigrants. Our public schools and universities have undermined our founders' objective of *E pluribus unum*, or "From many, one," that served us so well for almost two centuries. They have supplanted the practice of immigrants "assimilating" and becoming American and made diversity more important than social cohesion.

Rather than pushing cultural relativism, nonjudgmentalism, and multiculturalism on our children, we would be better served by exposing our children to many cultures; teaching them that diversity, social cohesion, and winning practices are all critical to their well-being; and teaching them to identify and adopt Winning Perspectives and Practices.

Declining Discipline, Poor Habits, and Less Learning

Greater general affluence, the unionization and liberalization of education, and the adoption of cultural relativism, multiculturalism, and nonjudgmentalism have caused parents and schools to be more permissive and less concerned about the habits children develop. The days of showing respect for one's elders, controlling emotional outbursts, and immediately responding to the directives of parents, teachers, and other authorities are passing. Not missing school, completing one's assignments on time, and doing well on a test the first time are no longer common expectations of parents and teachers.

We now have entered an era of little discipline, poor habits, and less learning. We hype our children's self-esteem, encourage them to vocalize their feelings, and let them do what they want. In doing this, we deny children the opportunity to learn self-control, to learn to defer gratification, and to form empowering habits. We set them up for a lifetime of disappointment rather than steady progress.

Oligopoly and Monopoly

When competition, free enterprise, and free markets prevail, buyers and sellers have choices, reputations matter, and people do the right things. When power concentrates, people and enterprises are less responsible and often become predatory.

Free enterprise and markets serve us well until a few buyers or sellers dominate a market. When sellers concentrate to the point where three or fewer sellers have most of the customers, buyers lose. Sellers overcharge, are unresponsive, and innovate less. Similarly, when buyers concentrate to the point where three or fewer make most of the purchases, sellers lose. Buyers underpay and dictate the transactional terms.

Over the years, we have seen monopoly and oligopoly with the railroads, energy providers, auto manufacturers, telephone companies, airlines, healthcare providers, cable companies, and numerous other industries. Each time a few companies dominate a market, consumers and suppliers lose. They have few alternatives and suffer economically.

Free enterprise and free markets only fail when governments permit a few buyers or sellers to dominate a market, when externalities exist, and on the rare occasions when human emotions cause extreme overselling. In such situations, prudent actions by governments and central banks can reduce market concentrations, mitigate the adverse effects of externalities and overselling, and restore the orderly function of enterprises and markets.

Offshoring

Starting in the 1960s, several companies found it advantageous to move their operations to Japan, Hong Kong, Singapore, South Korea, and Taiwan, and later in the 1980s, 1990s, and 2000s to China, Malaysia, and Vietnam. And rather than looking introspectively for the causes of the exodus, our leaders attributed the exodus to low-cost foreign labor.

While the low-cost labor in Asia has been a factor, there are numerous other causes of offshoring, such as high U.S. corporate tax rates, onerous government regulations, high levels of litigation, costly and uncooperative unions, and unaffordable health insurance. A 10 to 15 percent higher corporate income tax provides a serious incentive to locate elsewhere. Hundreds of thousands of pages of federal, state, and local government regulations, some of the most onerous in the world, significantly increase the cost of doing business in the U.S. Lots of regulations, lots of attorneys, and large pain and suffering award increased legal and insurance costs for businesses in our country. Private-sector unions have near monopolies on labor in some industries, and public-sector unions have absolute monopolies. These unions suppress productivity and directly and indirectly increase business costs in our country. And finally, healthcare, something many businesses provide, costs about one-third what businesses pay employees and twice as much in the U.S. than in most other countries.

While politicians and journalists blame the loss of American jobs, technology, and enterprise on inexpensive foreign labor, the truth is that our leaders' poor policy choices are primary causes. The unfriendly tax, regulatory, litigation, labor, and healthcare policies of the U.S., and the more business-friendly policies of other countries, incentivize companies to flee our shores.

Entitlement

The rapidly growing living standards of the 1940s and 1950s made most Americans feel fortunate. Social Security, unemployment insurance, and generous pension plans gave people a sense of financial security. This sense of prosperity and the social program green light from the Supreme Court enabled our representatives to pass a Disability Insurance program in the 1950s and Food Stamp, Medicare, Medicaid, and Welfare programs in the 1960s. America was so awesome that every citizen should live well.

Supporters of these programs wanted to help people, but they also wanted to increase their political power and win elections. They branded their opposition as heartless, removed the social stigma associated with public support, worked hard to sign people up for these programs, and won the day. The level of government that could best address poverty was not a consideration. The fact that most of these programs had not been piloted, they cost billions of dollars, and they tended to incentivize complacency were nonissues.

Before long, the days of believing that "we must earn our own way" gave way to "I deserve a good life" and then to "I have a right to a good life." Lee Kuan Yew, the founding father of Singapore and its prime minister from 1965 to 1990, understood the importance of avoiding entitlements and all their adverse effects. In just three decades, his leadership moved Singapore from Third World to First World. It transformed a poor, decrepit, crime-ridden city into a modern, affluent, orderly city-state that is perhaps the most livable city in the world. Statesmen and scholars the world over consider Lee Kuan Yew to have been one of the greatest leaders of the twentieth century, and his leadership and methods underlie many of China's recent successes. Commenting on the Western approach to poverty, he stated:

> American and European governments believed that they could always afford to support the poor and the needy: widows, orphans, the old and homeless, disadvantaged minorities, unwed mothers. Their sociologists expounded the theory that hardship and failure were due not to the individual person's character, but to flaws in the economic system. So charity became "entitlement," and the stigma of living on charity disappeared. Unfortunately, welfare costs grew faster than the government's ability to raise taxes to pay for it. The political cost of tax increases is high. Governments took the easy way out by borrowing to give higher benefits to the current generation of voters and passing the costs on to the future generations who were not yet voters.[21]

Entitlements and the political power associated with them are ruinous. They drive ever more spending, debt, wealth redistribution, and taxation, negatively affecting the people of every welfare state. They destroy people's incentives to learn, work, and save. They precipitate a loss of competitiveness and an eventual relative decline in living standards. Lest you think that I am heartless and do not recognize that many people need a little help, bear with me. I discuss the Winning Practices and what Lee Kuan Yew did to limit the need for entitlements and create a thriving population in *Winning Practices of a Free, Fit, and Prosperous People.*

Consumerism and Debt

The rapidly growing standards of living of the 1940s and 1950s and the cradle-to-grave social safety net of the 1960s caused Americans to loosen up. We saved less for the future, spent more freely, and borrowed more. The days of waiting until we had money to purchase something and saving for hardships and retirement ended for large portions of the population.

Americans had for decades used credit to finance their homes, but in the 1970s we started to purchase our cars with credit and to acquire credit cards. In the 1980s, we supplemented our lifestyles with credit cards, financing the purchase of our back-to-school clothes, birthday gifts, holiday gifts, televisions, and furniture. In the 1990s, we started borrowing to purchase houses that had twice the square footage of our parents' homes.

Throughout the 1980s, 1990s, and the first seven years of the 2000s, progressives pushed hard for low-income ownership of homes. They pressed banks to lower their lending standards. They pressured Freddie Mac and Fannie Mae, federally sponsored institutions, to support more and more low-income home ownership. People could purchase houses with no money down. People who had a negative net-worth and just enough income to make the payments on a thirty-year mortgage qualified for mortgages.

In the 1980s and 1990s, more and more Americans started to finance their college educations. Well-intended lawmakers facilitated this practice with the federally sponsored Sallie Mae institution. Sallie Mae eliminated most of the previously required qualifications for loans and offered students extremely lenient repayment terms. Now, seven in ten college students leave school with tens of thousands of dollars owed in student loans, and the federally sponsored system is almost insolvent.

What is the net effect of all this consumerism and debt? In 1964, total U.S. public and private debt was 1.1 trillion dollars. In 2015, it increased to 61.5 trillion dollars.[22] In 1964, some 60.2 million people were employed in our country. In 2015, approximately 157.8 million people were employed.[23] This works out to 17,600 dollars of debt per employed person in 1964 and $402,100 of debt per employed person in 2015. If we include the unfunded and underfunded commitments that federal, state, and local governments have made regarding public pensions, Social Security, Medicaid, Medicare, Disability, and healthcare, the picture is far worse.

When we consume mindlessly, save little, and borrow large sums, we live today at the expense of tomorrow. We have less investment income and pay more interest. Our government receives less tax revenue and pays more interest. We invest less in infrastructure, research, and development. Our productivity stagnates, and our competitiveness and living standards decline.

Easy Money

Easy money occurs when a country's central bank (1) decreases the amount of reserves commercial and retail banks must hold for each dollar they lend, (2) pays commercial and retail banks artificially low rates of interest to hold their money, or (3) buys its government's debt. Easy money distorts market prices. Enterprises and consumers borrow and spend more, causing the prices of goods, services, and assets to increase.

The easy money policies of the late 1990s and early 2000s set up the Great Recession of 2007–2009. Our central bank implemented easy money policies to avoid Y2K uncertainty and to stabilize the economy after the September 11 attacks. Afterward, they continued easy money policies to keep the good times rolling. Governments, enterprises, and consumers kept borrowing and spending. But demand for assets, goods, services, and debt cannot increase at increasing rates forever. Eventually, governments, enterprises, and consumers slow their purchases. When this occurs, as in 2008, prices and collateral values decrease. Like a receding tide exposes the beach, falling prices and collateral values expose excessive amounts of debt. They expose financial vulnerability, which often causes investors to panic.

Bear Stearns, Countrywide Financial, Fannie Mae, Freddie Mac, Goldman Sachs, Lehman Brothers, Merrill Lynch, and many other of the country's largest financial institutions had irresponsible levels of debt. To stem the ensuing panic and to restore order, the central bank implemented even more aggressive easy money policies in 2008 and for seven subsequent years. While an aggressive easy money policy was an appropriate response to the financial crisis, it was not appropriate to use so much in both the years preceding and following the crisis. And it was not appropriate for the central bank to purchase approximately two trillion dollars of U.S. debt between 2008 and 2014, essentially creating money out of thin air and keeping interest rates for commercial and retail banks under 0.25 percent through 2015.[24]

While easy money tempers economic contractions, it distorts market prices, decreases capital formation, and creates speculative bubbles. It steals purchasing power from savers and gives it to borrowers. It encourages governments, enterprises, and consumers to borrow and spend recklessly. Easy money is like heroin: Once central banks start using it, they cannot stop without causing a lot of pain and suffering.

Hubris and Nation Building

Hubris follows success. People become overconfident and less diligent. Success only leads to more success as we avoid hubris and as we keep learning, working, and doing our best. Hubris affects those who become intoxicated with their success and those who did not author their success. It often manifests itself in the children of successful generations who live large, develop a false sense of reality, and do not develop the necessary discipline, knowledge, work ethic, and judgment that enable success.

The change in the election of U.S. Senators, constitutional decoupling, promiscuity, the liberalism of education, relativism, multiculturalism, nonjudgmentalism, entitlement, consumerism, excessive debt, and easy money are manifestations of hubris. And to this list, we should add nation building. Having had tremendous success in helping Germany and Japan rebuild after WWII and South Korea after the Korean War, George W. Bush, Dick Cheney, Donald Rumsfeld, and others believed that we could depose any government and build a better one at will. What these leaders failed to recognize was that the Germans, Japanese, and South Koreans had as much to do with their success after WWII and the Korean War as we did. The Germans, Japanese, and South Koreans had a high prevalence of winning perspectives and practices within their cultures.

Attempts to nation build in Afghanistan and Iraq were doomed from the start. The Afghans and Iraqis have values that are incompatible with ours, and they have a much lower prevalence of winning practices within their populations. The cost of the misguided attempts to nation build in Afghanistan and Iraq in terms of treasure, life, and social cohesion have been staggering.

Immigration Failures

We have many immigration failures. Porous borders allow criminals, terrorists, and people who carry life-threatening diseases to enter the United States. Millions of illegal immigrants depress entry-level wages and make it harder for our citizens to find good-paying jobs. Many illegal immigrants do not know our language, do not share our values, have no prospects for employment, and will depend on public resources for the rest of their lives. Desirable immigrant applicants with needed work skills wait while illegal immigration divides our population and paralyzes our government. Immigrants concentrate in Southern California and South Florida, overwhelming the schools, health services, police forces, courts, jails, and social services in those areas.

Five percent of the U.S. population was foreign born in 1965 compared to 14 percent of the population, or approximately forty-five million people, in 2015.[25] In 1965, our families were more intact, our communities were safer, and our population was fitter. Real wages were increasing faster, proportionally fewer people were unemployed, and proportionally fewer people depended on the government. For the most part, we all spoke one language, our people were more unified, and we were less indebted.

Distorted News

One of the great unifying forces in our country was the existence of three or four national news outlets and two or three newspapers in most communities. The few national and local television, radio, and newspaper organizations incentivized their operators to uphold national and local community standards and appeal to all Americans.

With the advent of cable television, the Internet, and social media, the few national news organizations fragmented into numerous ones, and the local newspapers lost large portions of their advertising revenue. The fragmented national news organizations received revenue and audiences as they targeted their programming, appealed to our biases, and selectively reported and sensationalized the news, while many of the local news organizations went under. While more choice and customized services generally are desirable, this has not been the case with the news media. We now live in a world where most people only receive news that aligns with their biases and worldviews.

Political Polarization

Living in a country composed of people of multiple races, religions, and ethnic groups who live, attend school, and work in different communities tends to separate us. A federal legislature where half of the elected officials plus one enacts controversial laws, and where half of the population depends on social programs and the other half pays for them, further separates us. News organizations that reinforce this division by selectively reporting the news make it difficult for many people to even talk to each other.

American social cohesion is now as low as at any time in our history except for a few years during and after the Revolutionary, Civil, and Vietnam wars. People favor the protection of the unborn or a woman's right to choose. They favor the rule of law and legal immigration or porous borders and sanctuary cities. They favor less government, free market solutions, and lower taxes, or more social programs, more regulation, and higher taxes. They want or do not want the government to force us to reduce greenhouse gas emissions.

People assume positions that are common in their social circles. Fact-based, rational discussions are difficult. Common sense is rare. The practice of piloting policies and projects on a small scale and thoroughly examining their effects before their implementation on a large scale seldom occurs.

Separation from Nature

For some one hundred years, most Americans lived apart from nature and had only a cursory exposure to science. While we might visit a park or camp a few times a year, most of us occupy environments of wood, steel, concrete, glass, lawns, and pavement. Few of us have experience with large populations of plants and animals, savannahs, woodlands, jungles, deserts, frozen tundra, and oceans. Few of us sense our dependence upon our planet—its rhythms, climate, atmosphere, fresh water, soils, ecosystems, plants, and animals. Few of us appreciate the cycle of life—the coevolution of predators and prey and the importance of fitness.

We do not understand that we must compete, win, and have offspring, or we perish. We forget that we are vulnerable as individuals and much stronger as members of a family, community, and country. We do not distinguish between what we can change in our lifetime and what takes generations to change.

Our separation from nature and our limited understanding of science are unfortunate because there is so much perspective and wisdom within them. Affluence and technology give a license to live foolishly for a while, but eventually we will learn that our health, fitness, and well-being depend on nature and the alignment of our actions with it.

Losing Our Way

Inclusion Failures

The Change in the Election of U.S. Senators

Presidential Constitutional Failings

Supreme Court Constitutional Failings

Special Interest Government

Less Faith-Community Relevance

Less Integrity, Responsibility, and Civility

Promiscuity and the Decline of Marriage

Poorly Parented Children

Unionization of Education

Liberalization of Education

Social Justice Missteps

Cultural Relativism, Nonjudgmentalism, and Multiculturalism

Declining Discipline, Poor Habits, and Less Learning

Oligopoly and Monopoly

Offshoring

Entitlement

Consumerism and Debt

Easy Money

Hubris and Nation Building

Immigration Failures

Distorted News

Political Polarization

Separation from Nature

CHAPTER 2

Winning Perspectives

Winning Perspectives come to us from an understanding of the evolution of the universe, life, and culture. They help us identify Winning Practices from a murky sea of unlimited possibilities.

Singapore, Switzerland, and the United States

Of all the countries that I have visited and studied, Singapore and Switzerland have the largest proportions of their population flourishing. Before examining these countries, though, I will share a little background on Singapore. In 1940, Lee Kuan Yew, the eventual founder of the Republic of Singapore, graduated top in his class in the country. A few years later, after the Japanese occupation of Singapore, he studied law at Cambridge.

Singapore was as poor as Haiti in 1960. Drugs, gambling, and prostitution were widespread. Annual per-capita income was less than $425.[26] Racial riots were a major problem. Malaysia, concerned about the large Chinese population and dysfunction, abandoned Singapore in 1965. At this time, Lee Kuan Yew and his supporters took control of Singapore, implemented a strong rule of law, imprisoned political opposition, and cleaned up the mess. Today, Singapore has little problem with drugs relative to the U.S., has the sixth highest per-capita income in the world, has a thriving democracy, and is one of the greenest, most livable cities in the world.[27]

Switzerland, another of the most desirable places to live in the world, has a longer history than Singapore. Its history is more that of a people with a strong culture creating an outstanding government and institutions than that of a visionary leader creating a highly effective government and culture. Switzerland is interesting for many reasons, a few of which are their limited federal government, Executive Council, national referendums, and universal, affordable, high-quality healthcare.

Figure 4: Singapore, Switzerland, and the United States

	Singapore	Switzerland	USA
Country Characteristics			
Natural Resources	None	Few	Abundant
Major Languages	4	4	2
Population (millions)	6	8	320
Freedom and Opportunity			
Freedom Index Score (lower is freer)	43rd	2nd	20th
Economic Freedom Rank (lower is freer)	2nd	4th	16th
Youth Unemployment in 2015 (ages 15–24)	7.0%	8.3%	13.4%
Unemployment Rate in 2015	2.0%	3.3%	5.2%
Home Ownership Rate	90%	45%	65%
Quality of Government			
Country Corruption Rank (lower is less corrupt)	7th	5th	17th
Homicides (per 100,000 people)	0.2	0.6	4.7
Incarceration Rate (per 100,000 people)	220	85	700
Public Debt per Employed Person	$60,000	$32,000	$129,000
Foreign Exchange and Gold Reserves per Capita	$45,800	$73,000	$400
Family Function			
Adolescent Fertility Rate (births/1,000 women ages 15–19)	4	4	30
Divorces to Marriages per Year	28%	51%	53%
Population Replenishment (> 2.1 births/woman → growth)	1.3	1.5	1.9
Individual Well-Being			
Infant Mortality Rate	2.2%	3.5%	5.7%
Obesity Rate	7%	18%	33%
Portion of the Population with Health Insurance	100%	100%	88%
Health Expenditures as a Percent of GNP	5%	12%	17%
Life Expectancy at Birth (years)	82	83	79
Education			
Portion of the Population Completing High School	67%	86%	89%
Portion of Population Completing ≥ 2 Years of College	47%	37%	43%
Researchers (per million citizens)	6,300	5,000	3,840
Competitiveness and Income			
Tax Rate on Commercial Profits (before 2018)	18%	29%	44%
GDP per Capita 2015 (adjusted for purchasing power)	$82,300	$63,900	$55,600
GDP Increase over 55 Years	199x	33x	19x
Sustainability			
CO_2 Emissions per Capita (metric tons)	2.7	5.0	17.5
Mammal Species Threatened	10	2	35

The purpose of this chapter, though, is not to discuss Singaporean and Swiss government and institutions but to identify opportunities for improvement in our country and to learn where the methodologies for various improvements reside. Figure 4 compares life in Singapore, Switzerland, and the United States, and while we can learn much from many countries, Singapore and Switzerland offer some of the most important lessons.

Country Characteristics

Singapore's and Switzerland's living standards are stunning, given both countries have little developable real estate and few natural resources. Singapore's living standards are even more remarkable, considering it was as poor as Haiti in the 1960s, and the country didn't even have its own fresh water supply until recently.

Like our country, Singapore and Switzerland are multicultural. The Asian city-state of Singapore is primarily made up of Chinese, Malay, and Indians who speak English, Mandarin, Malay, or Tamil. Its principal religions include Buddhism, Islam, Hinduism, and Christianity. The small European country of Switzerland is composed of people with German, French, Italian, and Romansh heritages. Each of these groups speaks its own language, and most Swiss historically are either Roman Catholic or Protestant.

For decades, the Chinese dominated the Malays and Indians in Singapore, and the three groups did not get along well. In the 1960s, racial riots were common in Singapore. Ethnic and religious strife were also problems in Switzerland, where the Germans, Italians, French, Catholics, and Protestants did not get along well for centuries. Today, though, the Singaporeans and the Swiss make national cohesiveness a priority, work at it, and enjoy enviable cultural harmony.

While Singapore's and Switzerland's populations are only 6 million and 8 million people, respectively, compared to 320 million people in the U.S., their small size is not the cause of their success.[28] Rather, their success is a function of their leadership, their cultures, and the prevalence of Winning Practices within their populations. Leadership, culture, and Winning Practices are scalable.

Freedom and Opportunity

In 2015, Singapore, Switzerland, and the United States ranked forty-third, second, and twentieth, respectively, on the Cato Institute's Freedom Index and second, fourth, and seventeenth on their Economic Freedom Index.[29] While Singapore scores low on the overall Freedom Index relative to Switzerland and the U.S., it has been steadily improving its scores as the vestiges of the Lee Kuan Yew's dictatorship recede. Singapore and Switzerland both score much better than the U.S. on the Economic Freedom Index.

Youth unemployment runs 7.0, 8.6, and 13.4 percent in Singapore, Switzerland, and the U.S., respectively, while overall unemployment runs 2.0, 3.3, and 5.2 percent in the three countries.[30] Home ownership rates are 90 percent in Singapore, 45 percent in Switzerland, and 65 percent in the U.S.[31]

Singapore's home-ownership rate is the highest in the world. The winning practices of low tax rates and compulsory savings are responsible for it. These practices yield far more benefits to the population than the high income-tax rates, low savings rates, and wasteful government spending practices of Western countries. When people own their homes, they build equity as they age. They feel secure and good about themselves. They develop a tremendous pride in their neighborhoods and country. The winning practices of low tax rates and compulsory savings are completely untried in the West. I discuss them in detail in *The Winning Practices of a Free, Fit, and Prosperous People*.

Quality of Government

In the 1950s, the U.S. was considered one of the least corrupt and Singapore one of the most corrupt countries in the world. Now, according to Transparency International, the U.S. is dropping in the rankings, and Singapore and Switzerland both are less corrupt than the U.S.[32]

I would guess that most U.S. citizens who are fifty and older recognize the decline in honesty and lawfulness in our country. As I think back, most Americans outside the big cities felt no need to lock their homes or cars when I was young, and most students did not have or need lockers in school. When public officials lied or broke the law, they resigned from office and often went to jail. Such practices are rarer today, and their loss is not something we should accept, as corruption lowers living standards and quality of life.

The Western elite has nothing but disdain for Singapore's rule of law—more particularly, its use of fines and caning for noncriminal offenses and capital punishment for drug dealers. But unlike many Americans, Singaporeans live in safe neighborhoods, and they do not fear crime because it is so rare. Homicides average 0.2, 0.6, and 4.7 per 100,000 citizens in Singapore, Switzerland, and the U.S., respectively.[33] You are twenty-four times more likely to be murdered in the U.S. than in Singapore, and for many people living in several U.S. cities, the murder rate is several hundred times higher in the U.S. than Singapore. The U.S. incarcerates people at more than three times the rate of Singapore and more than eight times the rate of Switzerland.[34] The Singaporean and Swiss rule of law protects people, deters crime, keeps more families intact, and creates environments for people to flourish better than our rule of law.

Singapore and Switzerland have coexisted with powerful, hostile neighbors. While no one desires such neighbors, they sometimes yield positive effects. Powerful neighbors unify a country and often cause it to conscript and better enculturate young males, actions that typically strengthen the cohesiveness of its citizens and increase the prevalence of Winning Perspectives and Practices within its population.

Singapore and Switzerland take their defenses seriously. Men serve in the military or do public service and through such service become more disciplined. They acquire additional organizational, vocational, and intercultural skills. They learn to lead and follow at an early age, and they learn to live and work with all types of people. They develop a greater love for their country. And being small relative to other countries, the Singaporeans and the Swiss do not undertake expensive, divisive, lethal, and risky nation-building activities in other countries.

Singapore and Switzerland have more responsible governments than the U.S. The $60,000, $32,000, and $129,000 of public debt per employed person and the $45,800, $73,000, and $400 of foreign respective exchange and gold reserves per person are evidence of this.[35] Unlike the U.S., Singapore and Switzerland maintain balanced budgets, and their citizens form the capital that their economies require.

The Swiss modeled their government after our government but have not allowed their central government to assume so much power and become such a large part of their country's economy. The Swiss check their lawmakers by requiring a national referendum on many new federal laws and by allowing as few as fifty thousand Swiss citizens to force a referendum on any new law. Swiss parliament members serve part time, and they are less influenced by special interests than our representatives.

Family Function

Other striking comparisons among the three countries relate to family. Births per one thousand women ages fifteen to nineteen are four, four, and thirty, respectively, in Singapore, Switzerland, and the U.S.[36] This means that teenage pregnancy is seven to eight times more prevalent in the U.S. than in Singapore and Switzerland.

Divorces to marriages per year are 28 percent in Singapore, 51 percent in Switzerland, and 53 percent in U.S.[37] The more traditional family-related practices and less liberal welfare policies in Singapore, along with the greater opportunities for women in Switzerland and the U.S., account for much of the differences in the divorce rates.

All three countries have birth rates that do not sustain their populations and cultures. Singapore's and Switzerland's rates are the lowest.[38] All three countries must significantly raise their birth rates to 2.1 births per woman or make up their deficits with immigrants to sustain their populations.

Individual Well-Being

Infant mortality is 2.2, 3.5, and 5.7 percent in Singapore, Switzerland, and the U.S. respectively.[39] Seven percent of the population is obese in Singapore, 18 percent in Switzerland, and sadly, 33 percent in the U.S.[40] Obesity is a primary cause of diabetes, heart disease, cancer, premature death, and large medical bills. How can a people flourish when more than one-third of its population is obese?

In Singapore and Switzerland, 100 percent of the population is covered by health insurance. In the U.S., even after the Affordable Care Act, 88 percent of the population is covered.[41] Health expenditures as a percent of gross domestic product (GDP) per capita in Singapore, Switzerland, and the U.S. are 5, 12, and 17 percent, respectively.[42] Like Swiss healthcare, Singaporean healthcare is consumer-driven, of high quality, and a great value. In Singapore, life expectancy for men and women is 82 years, in Switzerland, 83 years, and in the U.S., 79 years.[43]

Education

Comparing education across the three countries reveals that while the U.S. once led the world in education, it has lost its edge in the last twenty years. The U.S. still graduates a larger proportion of its population from high school, but it no longer graduates a larger proportion from college. The higher U.S. high-school graduation rate also is misleading in the sense that large numbers of our students graduate without mastering the material.[44] Singapore, Switzerland, and many other countries have larger portions of their populations engaged in research than the U.S.[45]

Competitiveness and Income

Up until 2018, the U.S. tax on corporate profits of 44 percent was much higher than the rate of most other nations. Singapore's rate is 18 percent, and Switzerland's rate is 20 percent.[46] High corporate tax rates cause corporations to locate and take profits in other countries. This reduces the availability of higher paying U.S. jobs, lowers wages, and decreases U.S. tax revenues.

One can see the results of the varying prevalence of Winning Perspectives and Practices in the populations through the change in living standards over time. The GDP per capita is $82,300, $63,900, and $57,600 in Singapore, Switzerland, and the U.S., respectively.[47] In the last fifty-five years, living standards have increased 199 times in Singapore, 33 times in Switzerland, and only 19 times in the U.S.[48]

Sustainability

The U.S. pours far more climate-altering greenhouse gases into the atmosphere per capita than Singapore and Switzerland. Currently, we emit an estimated 17.5 tons of CO_2 per person, while the Singaporeans and Swiss emit only 2.7 and 5.0 tons per person.[49] Currently, the populations of Singapore, Switzerland, and the U.S. threaten ten, two, and thirty-five mammalian species, respectively.[50]

Winning Perspectives

Visiting and studying other countries makes us more realistic. Our perceptions become less imagined and more accurate. Working on a farm, running a business, practicing science, and investing, things I have spent a lot of time doing, also make us more realistic. One cannot cultivate large acreages, raise millions of animals, orchestrate significant business activities, explore cause-and-effect relationships, or earn a return on one's money without accurate perceptions of the world and assessments of the risks and benefits of various courses.

Most successful people, organizations, and governments ground their thought, decisions, and actions in reality. They learn from accomplished mentors. They gather evidence. They test hypotheses. They pilot new approaches on a small scale before committing resources on a large scale.

Under the leadership of Jack Welch, General Electric increased in market value forty times in just twenty years.[51] Welch attributes much of his and General Electric's success under his leadership to his mother's relentless emphasis on facing reality. He writes:

> The insights she drilled into me never faded. She always insisted on facing the facts of a situation. One of her favorite expressions was "Don't kid yourself. That's the way it is."[52]

I, too, favor reality, what works, and the perspectives and practices that enable us to flourish. Fashion, ideals, and political correctness do not interest me, as fashions are temporary, ideals are imagined states, and political correctness is a collection of a few people's political agendas.

Visiting and studying other countries expose us to the thoughts and practices of other people and make us more insightful about others' and our own country's practices. These activities jar us, free us from groupthink, expose opportunities, and indicate where we can find better methodologies.

Science and the study of the universe, earth, and life also bring tremendous perspective. They expand our physical and time horizons and enable us to see otherwise inaccessible views of the universe, earth, life, and natural processes. Reality is as it is and not as we wish it to be.

From such study, I have found the perspectives of Truth, Causality, Scale, Evolution, Fitness, Human Nature, Periodic Disaster, and Eco-Dependency to be especially helpful, so helpful in fact that I call them Winning Perspectives and devote the remainder of the book to them. What are Winning Perspectives?

Winning Perspectives—*accurate perceptions of reality and the conditions of existence.*

Substantial evidence for Winning Perspectives exists. Winning Perspectives further our effectiveness. They provide direction, and most importantly, they help us identify the Winning Practices that enable us to flourish.

CHAPTER 3

Truth

The truth is incontrovertible. Malice may attack it, ignorance may deride it, but in the end, there it is.[53]

—*Winston Churchill*

The first of the eight Winning Perspectives is truth. I define truth as accurate approximations of reality, natural processes, and events, and while truth is understandable in concept, it is elusive in practice.

Things just are not always what they seem. For proof of this, simply step outside and gaze as far as your surroundings permit. It's no surprise that for thousands of years our ancestors thought the earth was flat, as this is the way it appears when we're standing on it. But this is not the truth, as images of Earth from space show us. Limited perspective, the invisibility of many cause-and-effect relationships, self-interest bias, spin, and groupthink all distort our perceptions.

As with the flatness of the earth, generally we do not perceive a truth until we see something from several vantage points. Children and professional magicians see magic differently. Children see the illusion. Magicians see the illusion, artistry, and deception. Children and magicians see the same performance, but magicians see it with experience, from more vantage points, and with more accuracy.

Our perceptions of our world take place on a very limited scale—a few years, one-hundredth of an inch, a few miles, and only as they directly affect us. Without science and technology, much is invisible to us. With science and technology, we see galaxies, solar systems, microscopic life, molecules, atoms, and interactions on large and small scales. I discuss science and the scientific method in detail in *Winning Practices of a Free, Fit, and Prosperous People.*

Grasping truth is difficult because our ego and our self-interest color our perceptions. Generally, we want to be "right" more than we want to be "accurate," and we see events as it is in our interest to see them. If we espouse or invest in a position, we are more often defending it than quietly listening to others and learning from them. If we collide with a car at a four-way stop, most of us will blame the other driver. If one of our children is involved in a fight, most of us will fault the other child unless our child has a history of fighting.

People also do not communicate truthfully. We want others to see us in a positive light. We mask our interests and create narratives, telling others what we want them to hear and what we think they want to hear. Children spin stories for their parents, politicians for their constituents, and subordinates for their superiors, and vice versa. Unless we have a strong truth-telling ethic, we shade the truth rather than tell it.

Evolution has wired us to absorb others' thinking. This tendency served us well as hunter-gathers for millions of years but less well in the modern world. This tendency facilitates social cohesion but hinders our ability to make a complex civilization work. As inventor extraordinaire Thomas Edison wrote:

> If we bother with facts at all, we hunt like bird dogs after the facts that bolster up what we already think—and ignore all the others! We want only the facts that justify our acts—the facts that fit in conveniently with [our] wishful-thinking and justify our preconceived prejudices![54]

"We also see things not as they are but as we are," as the maxim goes. Whether Republican, Democrat, Caucasian, Hispanic, African American, Jewish, Christian, or Muslim, each of us does this. The views of those with whom we associate take root in our unconscious. If we learned at a young age in the eighteenth century that Native Americans were heathen murderers, we would hide from them and probably shoot those who strayed onto our property. We would completely miss the fact that the Indians loved their children, enjoyed their families and communities, and just wanted to retain their lives and lands. Carl Sagan wrote:

> The truth may be puzzling. It may take some work to
> grapple with. It may be counterintuitive. It may contra-
> dict deeply held prejudices. It may not be consonant with
> what we desperately want to be true. But our preferences
> do not determine what's true.[55]

In a sense, our views always are becoming like those with whom we spend the most time. If our social circle is primarily composed of conservatives, we will see the government as inefficient, wasteful, and restrictive. If it is primarily composed of liberals, we will see government as a helpful tool to eliminate prejudice and inequality. We recognize groupthink as outsiders of groups but not as insiders.

Our tendency to absorb others' thinking is greatest when we are children and our minds are open to the views of our parents, older siblings, teachers, and coaches. It is also strong in our teens when an intense desire to "fit in" opens our minds to our peers. Then our malleable minds harden sometime in our mid-twenties when our routines, peers, and groups stabilize. We register information that reinforces our views and ignore information that challenges them. Others' views affect us but on a much more limited basis, as mature brains do not easily substitute new views for old ones.

While science provides the best method to discern truth, sometimes the truth eludes even scientists. Newton's laws of motion provide a good example of this, and their history underscores the importance of avoiding certitude. Every observation and experiment confirmed Newton's laws of motion for two hundred years, but then Einstein realized that they only approximate reality at familiar scales, and they are incorrect at large and small scales. Carl Sagan wrote:

Humans may crave absolute certainty; they may aspire to it; they may pretend, as partisans of certain religions do, to have attained it. But the history of science—by far the most successful claim to knowledge accessible to humans—teaches that the most we can hope for is successive improvement in our understanding.[56]

Because so much works against our perception of truth, and because truth underlies our effectiveness, we must appreciate those who discern and express it. Leaders, authorities, famous people, and those engaged in science, research, and teaching have a special responsibility to communicate truthfully, as their views affect so many other people. Imagine the harm done if doctors told their patients that smoking poses no risk or teachers told their less diligent students that they were stupid.

Truth hides from us, and human nature distorts it. Our initial perceptions are only a start in our quest for truth. We must ponder our perceptions, read, travel, verify what others tell us, solicit different views, conduct experiments, and gather evidence. Increasing amounts of varied evidence improves our perceptions, makes us iteratively more intelligent, and makes our solutions iteratively more effective.

Truth—*accurate approximations of reality, natural processes, and events.*

CHAPTER 4

Causality

Behind every event is one or more causes.

We have poorly understood the cause-and-effect nature of the universe for most of history, as most causes are invisible to us. For thousands of years, we thought capricious acts of gods, God, wizards, and witches caused diseases, pestilence, and famine. Not until Robert Hooke and others had the benefit of the microscope did we learn that bacteria cause diseases. Not until we understood the gestation cycles of insects did we discover the cause of pestilence. Only when we learned about the effects that massive volcanic eruptions had on temperatures did we recognize that they were major causes of famine.

Without telescopes, microscopes, and other sensory aids, most of the universe and natural processes are imperceptible to us. Cosmic structure and distances, the fusion of the atoms, DNA's orchestration of life, and cell division are undetectable. Without sensory aids, knowledge of stars, general relativity, and the multibillion-year sequence of events that shaped the universe would be out of our reach. Without the fossil record, careful observation, and imagination, we could not grasp the evolution of life and the cumulative effects of innumerable small changes that occur over thousands of generations.

Thousands of scientists have spent hundreds of years exposing the 13.7-billion-year sequence of causes and effects that shaped the universe and life. Although scientists have numerous details still to work out, they have deciphered a great deal. Understanding that there are one or more causes for every event is a giant step forward for sapiens. Ceasing to attribute events to gods, God, wizards, witches, bad luck, and others' ill intentions, and knowing the real causes of them, improves our quality of life immensely.

I learned quickly on the farm and in business that understanding the cause or causes of problems is crucial. When we do not address the causes of problems, the problems remain. Alleviating the symptoms of problems makes us feel better, but it does not eliminate the problems.

Consider the challenge of providing clean drinking water to a community where the only adequate source of water is a lake high in phosphates and nitrates. The municipality has two common choices: (1) require landowners to put in vegetation buffers and retention ponds around the lake to manage runoff from their properties, or (2) treat the water to reduce the phosphates and nitrates to acceptable levels. The first approach has a high initial cost, eliminates the contamination, and forever solves the problem. The second approach has a low initial cost, high ongoing costs, and does not eliminate the problem. Which is the better solution? While the answer to this question depends on the severity of the adverse effects and the costs and benefits of the alternative approaches over time, eliminating the causes of problems and being rid of the problems forever is usually superior to treating their symptoms.

Fallacy, Correlation, Necessity, and Sufficiency

When thinking about causes and their effects, understanding the concepts of fallacy, correlation, necessity, and sufficiency is helpful.

A **Fallacy** is the incorrect attribution of cause to effect.

"You will catch a cold if you go outside with wet hair" is a fallacy. It is a fallacy because viruses cause colds, not wet hair. "Government may lower the cost of healthcare by setting the prices for it" is a fallacy, as price fixing does nothing to lower the costs of providing healthcare. Price fixing merely decreases the number of providers and increases the time people wait for the services offered by lower-cost and/or poorer-quality providers. Fallacies are more common than we realize. They occur when people are ignorant and unaccountable, and superstition prevails.

Correlation is the simultaneous occurrence of two events.

Correlation does not imply causation. It implies coincidence. Correlations may be random, causal, or joint products of some event. One of the most common fallacies is to believe a correlation between two events implies a causal relationship.

Consider a hypothetical health study that finds a correlation between eating organic foods and a lower incidence of colds. Does the correlation mean that eating organic foods lowers the incidence of colds? No, the correlation does not tell us this. The association of eating organic foods and fewer colds only indicates that the two events are coincident. The correlation could result from the phenomenon that people eating organic foods have fewer children and, therefore, less exposure to cold viruses. If this were the case, eating organic foods would coincide with having fewer colds, but it would not lower incidences of colds, as exposure to the viruses that children carry causes colds.

Logicians and scientists distinguish the causes or conditions related to an event as contributory, necessary, or sufficient.

A **Contributory Condition** is a circumstance that plays a role in producing an effect.

A **Necessary Condition** is a circumstance that must be present to produce an effect.

Sufficient Conditions are the complete set of circumstances that must be present to produce an effect.

Regular exercise is a contributory condition of good health. It furthers good health but does not assure it. Some people have good health with or without it. Regular training is a necessary condition of winning a marathon. Entrants do not win marathons without it, but it alone does not assure victory. Running full speed into a concrete wall is a sufficient condition to harm oneself. The act alone guarantees harm.

Of these three types of conditions, sufficiency is the most interesting. Sufficiency refers to the set of conditions that produce an effect. Knowing the set is powerful. The conditions for sufficiency, like most cause-and-effect relationships, are usually invisible and difficult to determine, but we may discover them with careful observation and experimentation. Science excels in determining the sufficient conditions for events. Consider a simplified summary of what scientists have learned about our universe by way of observation, experimentation, and understanding the sufficient conditions of natural processes.

In the fractions of a second after the start of the universe, elementary subatomic particles formed. As the universe cooled, the motion and density of these particles became just right to cause the formation of the nuclei of simple atoms, like hydrogen, helium, and deuterium. As the universe cooled more, the motion and density of these nuclei and free electrons formed simple atoms. As the universe cooled some more, the slower motion and greater densities of these simple atoms allowed them to aggregate.

The aggregation of atoms creates gravity, pressure, and heat. Where enough hydrogen, helium, and deuterium aggregate and gravity creates temperatures in excess of twenty-five million degrees Kelvin, simple atoms fuse, and stars ignite. Two hydrogen protons form a deuterium nucleus and eject a positron and neutrino in the process. Large stars fuse the deuterium nuclei and heavier nuclei into all the elements on the periodic table up to iron. Then, as the largest of these stars exhaust their supplies of these lighter elements, they collapse and explode, creating pressures and temperatures that fuse the heavier elements.

Some of the exploded debris assembles into molecules or collections of atoms that share electrons. One carbon and two oxygen atoms assemble into carbon dioxide. One nitrogen and three hydrogen atoms form ammonia. One oxygen and two hydrogen atoms form water.

The debris made up of light elements, heavy elements, and molecules coalesce into planets, asteroids, comets, and new stars. Comets of ice bombard planets, and liquids pool and evaporate. Planetary seas and atmospheres form. With the right combination of gases, liquids, temperature, and molecules, some of the molecules assemble into nucleotides and amino acids. Scientists replicate nucleotide and amino acid self-assembly in test tubes.

Currently, scientists are trying to determine the sufficient conditions for basic proteins to self-assemble into RNA. These conditions may have existed near alkaline vents deep within the seas some 3.8 billion years ago. If this was the case, the basic proteins and RNA most likely formed DNA and eventually one or more cells. One or more of the cells divided, and the daughter cells divided again. Then, the DNA in the cells and natural selection orchestrated the formation of every cell, plant, and animal. Evidence for this possibility mounts as scientists learn the sufficient conditions for the process.

The Inanimate and Animate Worlds

Not long ago, we did not know about these conditions, processes, and events. We thought the heavens, earth, and life were the handiwork of gods or God. The processes occurred on such a small scale, so far away, and so long ago that we did not perceive them. Knowing the sufficient conditions of effects and events is ever more helpful.

Just as things happen at the atomic and cellular levels given the right conditions, so they happen at the organism and superorganism levels. The only difference is that higher animals inject some unpredictability into events. Higher animals make choices.

For example, when someone is mean to us, usually we reciprocate meanness if we are strong, and we flee if we are weak. People's relative strength affects others' treatment of us and our responses. Sometimes we may suppress our instinctual responses to retaliate or flee and respond with kindness. This is not a natural response but a choice. Sufficient conditions for an event at the atomic and cellular levels are much more straightforward than those at the human level.

"We reap as we sow"—a reality that we receive in accordance to what we do—is a causality that generally holds. Others compensate us as we work. Others assist us as we assist them, and others harm us as we harm them. While we may not always receive our due in the short term, we frequently do in the long term.

The causality perspective teaches us that events are not arbitrary. When conditions are sufficient, things happen. Simple elements assemble into heavier elements; combinations of elements assemble into molecules; some molecules assemble into amino acids; amino acids assemble into proteins; and proteins assemble into RNA, DNA, and cells. Cells divide, differentiate, and form single and multicell life-forms. The sufficient conditions for these processes and events occur innumerable times each day on earth and most likely throughout the universe.

The invisible nature of causal relationships blinds us to the effects of many of our actions. Mentors, experts, science, and experience, especially when we are young, expose the long-term effects of our actions and help us act more prudently, and herein is a perspective and practice that all children should learn.

Our world is comprehensible. The cause-and-effect relationships are predictable at the atomic and cellular levels and largely predictable at the human level. Our beliefs, prayers, and preferences do not alter these causal relationships. They may affect our behavior and people's responses to our behaviors, but they do not change causal relationships. As historians, philosophers, and authors Will and Ariel Durant wrote in their eleven-volume *The Story of Civilization:*

> In the end, nothing is lost. Every event, for good or evil, has effects forever.[57]

The thirty-six Winning Practices that I discuss in the *Flourish* Series do not describe all the sufficient conditions for people to flourish, but they describe many of them. Hopefully, my attempt to delineate some of the most important ones will encourage others to describe more of the sufficient conditions for human fitness and well-being.

Causality—*the reality that every effect has one or more causes.*

CHAPTER 5

Scale

Fleeting specks of dust are we—transient and minute relative to the age and scope of the universe.

Our understanding of the universe, the composition of matter, and time has expanded so much over the last five hundred years. Five hundred years ago, we understood distances as small as the thickness of a human hair, or about 10^{-4} meters, and distances as great as a thirty-day horseback ride, or about 10^6 meters. Today, we understand distances as small as one Planck length, or about 10^{-35} meters, and as large as our universe of about 10^{27} meters.

Just a few centuries ago, we understood masses as small as a mosquito of 10^{-6} kilograms and as large as an ocean-going ship of 10^5 kilograms. Today, we understand masses as small as an electron of 10^{-32} kilograms and as large as a galaxy of 10^{42} kilograms.

Five hundred years ago, we had a sense of one hundred human generations, or two thousand years. Today we think in terms of millions of human generations and billions of years. Figure 5: Small and Large Distances, Figure 6: Small and Large Masses, and Figure 7: Evolution of the Universe and Life Timeline delineate the scale of our current perspectives.

As our understanding of the scale of distance, mass, and time expands, so does our understanding of our place in the universe. Five hundred years ago, we thought the earth was flat and God created everything for our benefit. We thought we had dominion over the planet and other life-forms. Now, we understand that we live in one of the more than two trillion galaxies, orbit around one of the more than one billion stars in our galaxy, and live on one of the billions of potentially hospitable planets in the universe. We realize that all earthly life-forms descend from a common life-form, we are the products of over three billion years of natural selection, and we may become a dead leaf on the evolutionary tree or a branch to hundreds, thousands, or even millions of generations of life.

Our views of the universe and life have changed so much in the last twenty generations. Now the universe seems endlessly divisible and expansive, and life incredibly complex! The universe and life are wondrous and dazzling! As naturalist and Pulitzer Prize–winner Annie Dillard writes:

> After the one extravagant gesture of creation in the first place, the universe has continued to deal exclusively in extravagances, flinging intricacies and colossi down eons of emptiness, heaping profusions on profligacies with ever-fresh vigor. The whole show has been on fire from the word go. I come down to the water to cool my eyes. But everywhere I look I see fire; that which isn't flint is tinder, and the whole world sparks and flames.[58]

Scale—*understanding that the magnitudes of distance, mass, and time in the universe are very different from those we experience every day and realistically grasping our place in the universe.*

Figure 5: Small and Large Distances

English Description (Meters)	Metric Name	Number (Meters)	Scientific Notation (Meters)
Planck Length — 0.16 trillionth trillionth trillionths		0.000,000,000,000,000,000,000,000,000,000,000,016	1.6×10^{-35}
Electron Diameter — 5.6 millionth billionths	5.6 femtometers	0.000,000,000,000,0056	5.6×10^{-15}
Hydrogen Diameter — 5.0 trillionths	5.0 picometers	0.000,000,000,005	5.0×10^{-12}
Smallest Transistor Gate — 2.5 billionths	2.5 nanometers	0.000,000,0025	2.5×10^{-9}
Red Blood Cell Diameter — 7.0 millionths	7.0 micrometers	0.000,007	7.0×10^{-6}
Human Hair Diameter — 0.1 thousandths	0.1 millimeters	0.000,1	0.1×10^{-3}
Moon's Diameter — 3.5 million	3.5 megameters	3,500,000	3.5×10^{6}
Earth's Diameter — 12.8 million	12.8 megameters	12,800,000	12.8×10^{7}
Sun's Diameter — 1.4 billion	1.4 gigameters	1,400,000,000	1.4×10^{9}
Earth to the Sun — 150.0 billion	150.0 gigameters	150,000,000,000	150.0×10^{9}
Sun to Pluto — 5.9 trillion	5.9 terameters	5,900,000,000,000	5.9×10^{12}
One Light Year — 9.5 quadrillion	9.5 petameters	9,500,000,000,000,000	9.5×10^{15}
Earth to Proxima Centauri — 39.9 quadrillion	39.9 petameters	39,900,000,000,000,000	39.9×10^{15}
Milky Way Diameter — 1.0 billion trillion	1.0 zeptometers	1,000,000,000,000,000,000,000	1.0×10^{21}
Universe Diameter — 920.0 trillion trillion	920.0 yottameters	920,000,000,000,000,000,000,000	920.0×10^{24}

Orders of Magnitude, Wikipedia,
http://en.wikipedia.org/wiki/Orders_of_magnitude_(length)

Figure 6: Small and Large Masses

	English Description (Grams)	Metric Name	Number (Grams)	Scientific Notation (Grams)
Electron	0.9 thousandth trillionth trillionths		0.000,000,000,000,000,000,000,000,0009	0.9×10^{-27}
Hydrogen Atom	1.7 trillionth trillionths	1.7 yoctograms	0.000,000,000,000,000,000,000,0017	1.7×10^{-24}
Small Protein	55.0 billionth trillionths	55.0 zeptograms	0.000,000,000,000,000,000, 055	55.0×10^{-21}
Human Sperm Cell	22.0 trillionths	22.0 picograms	0.000,000,000,022	22.0×10^{-12}
Average Human Cell	1.0 billionths	1.0 nanograms	0.000,000,001	1.0×10^{-9}
Human Ovum	3.6 millionths	3.6 micrograms	0.000,0036	3.6×10^{-6}
Mosquito	2.5 thousandths	2.5 milligrams	0.025	2.5×10^{-3}
Blue Whale	200.0 million	200.0 megagrams	200,000,000	200.0×10^{6}
Human Population	400.0 trillion	400.0 teragrams	400,000,000,000,000	400×10^{12}
Moon	73.0 trillion trillion	73.0 yottagrams	73,000,000,000,000,000,000,000,000	73×10^{24}
Earth	6.0 trillion quadrillion		6,000,000,000,000,000,000,000,000,000	6.0×10^{27}
Sun	2.0 billion trillion trillion		2,000,000,000,000,000,000,000,000,000,000,000	2.0×10^{33}
Milky Way Black Hole	8.0 trillion trillion quadrillion			8.0×10^{39}
Milky Way Galaxy	1.2 billion trillion trillion trillion			1.2×10^{45}
Universe	2.0 trillion trillion trillion trillion quadrillion			2.0×10^{63}

Orders of Magnitude, Wikipedia,
http://en.wikipedia.org/wiki/Orders_of_magnitude_(mass)

Figure 7: Evolution of the Universe and Life Timeline

	Millennia Ago	Generations (25 yrs.)	Years Ago
The Big Bang	13,700,000		13,700,000,000
Nucleosynthesis	13,700,000		13,700,000,000
Star Formation	13,200,000		13,200,000,000
Milky Way Galaxy Formation	8,800,000		8,800,000,000
Solar System Formation	4,600,000		4,600,000,000
Simple Cells	3,600,000		3,600,000,000
Photosynthesis	3,000,000		3,000,000,000
Complex Cells	2,000,000		2,000,000,000
Sexual Reproduction	1,200,000		1,200,000,000
Multicellular Life	1,000,000		1,000,000,000
Fish	500,000		500,000,000
Land Plants	475,000		475,000,000
Insects	400,000		400,000,000
Amphibians	360,000		360,000,000
Reptiles	300,000		300,000,000
Mammals	200,000		200,000,000
Birds	150,000		150,000,000
Primates	75,000	3,000,000	75,000,000
Hominini	7,000	280,000	7,000,000
Homo Erectus	1,800	72,000	1,800,000
Homo Sapiens	200	8,000	200,000
Mitochondrial Eve	150	6,000	150,000
Y-Chromosomal Adam	140	5,600	140,000
Human Migration to South Asia	50	2,000	50,000
Human Migration to Europe and Australia	40	1,600	40,000
Domestication of the Wolf/Dog	15	600	15,000
Beginning of Agriculture	10	400	10,000
Beginning of the Calendar	2	80	2,000
Beginning of the United States	0	9	233

Chronology of the Universe, Wikipedia, http://en.wikipedia.org/wiki/Chronology_of_the_universe

Timeline of the Evolutionary History of Life, Wikipedia,
http://en.wikipedia.org/wiki/Timeline_of_the_evolutionary_history_of_life

Timeline of Human Evolution, Wikipedia, http://en.wikipedia.org/wiki/Timeline_of_human_evolution

CHAPTER 6

Evolution

What an amazing story! What elegant simplicity! Variation, competition, and the continuation of what works and the discontinuation of what doesn't work over and over again!

Like the first few seconds of the universe, the origin of the first cell and life is murky. Scientists know that the early earth was a hot, radioactive, and violent place. Asteroids and comets bombarded the planet with radioactive debris and water from earlier supernova explosions.[59] Gases from the debris and evaporation formed our atmosphere, and water from the comets formed our oceans. Given the available molecules, the early atmosphere would have been a mix of hydrogen, nitrogen, oxygen, carbon, carbon monoxide, carbon dioxide, and hydrogen sulfide, and the oceans would have been quite acidic.[60]

Then, some four billion years ago, after the earth's crust cooled, conditions were right for the building blocks of life to self-assemble.[61] Scientists find amino acids, nucleobases, phospholipids, and RNA templates naturally form when they replicate these conditions, but they have yet to resolve how the building blocks of life became DNA, protocells, and the first cell. Life originating in space and finding its way to Earth is a possibility, but the leading theory is that life originated deep in the ocean near a hydrothermal vent and that when conditions are just right, DNA and protocells form.[62]

Scientists know that once cellular life started, mutations, sex, and recombination varied cellular traits. The organisms that survive and reproduce increase the frequency of their kind and heritable traits. Drawing resources from the environment, they transform the resources and deposit the transformations back into the environment. The environment acts on life, life acts on the environment, and the interaction changes the mix of traits that enables continued success. This ever-so-slow iterative interaction creates all the life-forms on earth and transforms the Earth itself in the process.

Mutations are changes in DNA sequences. They result from large sections of a chromosome duplicating and inserting into a gene, or small parts of several genes duplicating, recombining, and finding their way into a gene.[63] Ultraviolet radiation causes mutations, and it was much more intense when life started three to four billion years ago than it is today.[64] Sex and recombination involve the unraveling of two parents' chromosomes and a mixed recombination of them. Sex and recombination do not alter trait frequencies within gene pools, but they do produce offspring with new combinations of chromosomes.

One of the first organisms, the chemoautotrophs, used carbon dioxide to oxidize inorganic materials approximately 3.5 billion years ago. A little later, prokaryotes evolved. Prokaryotes free energy from organic molecules and store it as ATP, a process utilized in almost all organisms today. Photosynthesizing cyanobacteria evolved three billion years ago. They produce oxygen, and their arrival caused oxygen levels in the atmosphere to rise. Eukaryotic cells, membrane-bound organelles with diverse functions, appeared some 1.8 billion years ago.[65]

The evolution of life accelerated with the rise of sexual reproduction approximately 1.2 billion years ago. Sexual reproduction creates more variation among offspring than mutations alone do. The traits that aid survival are "naturally selected" in the environment and over time become more prevalent in the population's gene pool.

Protozoa emerged as little as one billion years ago. Enough oxygen accumulated in the atmosphere to form the ozone layer, shielding the earth from much of the deadly ultraviolet radiation and enabling life to emerge on land some 580 million years ago. The earliest fungi evolved approximately 560 million years ago, the first vertebrates 485 million years ago, the first plants on land 434 million years ago, the first insects 363 million years ago, the first amphibians 340 million years ago, and the first reptiles 305 million years ago. The first dinosaurs appeared 225 million years ago, the first flowering plants 130 million years ago, and the first ants 80 million years ago. The earliest mammals arrived

30 million years ago, apelike animals 2 million years ago, Neanderthals 350,000 years ago, and modern humans 200,000 years ago.[66]

At least 3.5 billion years have passed since life's beginning. To gain a sense of a billion years, consider that one hundred human generations span two thousand years, while fifty million human generations span a billion years. From the fossil records, carbon dating, and DNA records, scientists estimate that humans evolved from a more primitive species some four hundred thousand years ago, or twenty thousand generations ago.[67] Four hundred thousand years represents less than 0.01 percent of the 3.5-billion-year period.

Today each of us is alive because of the successful struggle of some twenty thousand generations of human ancestors, as well as the successful struggles of all the species from which humans descended. To think we are the result of 13.7 billion years of the universe's evolution and over 3.5 billion years of protocell, cell, organism, and species struggle is mind boggling, ennobling, and humbling. Just pondering the viruses, bacteria, and natural predators that the twenty thousand generations of our human ancestors overcame makes one realize how consequential some battles are and how long their effects ripple through time.

A study of the evolution of life reveals scientists' detailed understanding of most of the four-billion-year sequence of events. When we carefully consider scientists' narratives and are not blinded by contrary belief, we find their explanations are understandable, and the evidence for them is consistent, persuasive, and overwhelming. Widely accepted scientific explanations for the evolution of life are supported by (a) the fossil record, (b) the anatomical and time-related progression of species, (c) selective breeding experiences, (d) experimental data from all branches of science on evolutionary processes, (e) cellular commonality, and (f) the progression of DNA sequences.

Competition and Comparative Advantage

Competition drives evolution. It winnows the slackers from the enterprising, the weak from the strong, the losers from the winners. It determines whose progeny and genes continue; whose perspectives, practices, and priorities continue; and which schools, universities, enterprises, governments, and countries continue.

Competitions force organisms and organizations to perform. They force them to learn, prepare, work hard, and innovate. They cause people to give their best efforts. Without competitions, people take advantage of their positions, shirk responsibility, and freeload.

When leaders and organizations dominate a people, region, or market, they do not perform as well as when their constituents or customers have alternatives. This is true for enterprises, schools, political parties, governments, religions, and countries. Alternatives create competition and encourage performance.

Though some participants in competitions lose, comparative advantage assures there are opportunities for everyone. The comparative advantage insight originates in economics and explains the benefits of trade between countries.

> **Comparative Advantage** is the reality that when individuals or countries specialize and trade, each doing what he, she, or it does best, each party benefits. Even when one party does everything more efficiently than the other party, each party benefits from specializing, selling some output, and using the proceeds to purchase what others do best.

Comparative advantage makes competition palatable. When we lose in one arena, we can succeed in other ones. If we do not make the high school basketball team, we may make the swim or volleyball teams, or if we are artistic, we might sing in the chorus, play in the band, or act in a theater production.

Even though some people might do all these activities better than us, they do not have time to do them all. If we search and persist, we find opportunities. Competition condemns no one to ongoing failure. Only resignation—something in our control—perpetuates failure. Because we do not have the time and strength to enter all competitions, and our opportunity to win some of them is greater than others, judicious selection of competitions improves our likelihood of success.

In most competitions, both the winners and losers benefit as the preparation strengthens the participants. When we compete for a job and do not receive it, we improve our job interviewing skills. When we compete for a position that requires training and certification and do not receive it, we benefit from the training and certification.

We also reap more from competition than our individual winnings. Competition allocates positions and resources to those who most ably use them. It causes all levels of human organization to function better. When we award positions in a competitive manner and only retain those who perform well, the ablest people lead and occupy the positions in our organizations. CEOs who competitively earn their positions are the ones most likely to make their organizations flourish. Teachers who competitively win their positions are the best instructors. Police officers who competitively earn their positions are the ones most able to keep our neighborhoods safe. We benefit from all these competitions in the form of the better-functioning schools, enterprises, communities, and governments, even if we do not win any of the competitions.

Need stimulates our appetite for competition. Affluence diminishes it. Poorer people and populations rise, and affluent ones decline. When poor people do not have comfortable social safety nets, a little work improves their lives much more than it improves affluent people's lives.

Although few of us consider it, competition supports our free enterprise system and representative democracy. We form our views from the information we receive from competing news organizations. We select our products and services from arrays of competing ones. We choose our elected officials from slates of competing candidates, and our representatives select our policies from numerous competing ones.

Without competition, leaders, political parties, journalists, and scientists do not have sufficient incentive to challenge one another's self-serving actions and inaction. They are less honest, do not work as hard, and do not innovate as much. Those assigning jobs give them to their friends rather than to the best-suited applicants. Incompetent people become leaders, researchers, doctors, engineers, and teachers. Inefficiency increases, little works well, and living standards decline. While competition is hard on some individuals, history demonstrates repeatedly that its benefits outweigh all other alternatives.

This insight warrants wider circulation and greater appreciation. Competitions improve the effectiveness of our organizations, enterprises, and government. They make us fitter, lower the costs of goods and services, and improve the accuracy of our views and the quality of our lives.

And despite what some people say, competition among countries need not result in war. Countries can compete with one another and peacefully coexist when they (a) have access to needed resources, (b) stabilize their population growth, (c) maintain physical, technological, financial, and military fitness, and (d) have healthy inter-country relationships. We need only look to the Swiss to see how this is done. In the middle of war-torn Europe, the Swiss have lived peacefully for more than 150 years, and they have done this by satisfying these conditions.

> **Competition** is (a) two or more ideas, practices, or things competing for some form of superiority, or (b) two or more organisms battling for territory, resources, mates, influence, and existence.

While the best leaders, teachers, coaches, and parents may choose to shield our youngest children from competition for four to five years, they otherwise embrace it. They understand that competition creates individual, organizational, and population excellence; competition is the most objective, fair, and effective method for allocating resources and positions and deciding which, who, and what advances; and comparative advantage assures there are opportunities for everyone.

Natural Selection and Gradualism

Before the 1800s, no one imagined that life was the handiwork of a simple natural process and billions of years. Natural selection, undetectable in one generation, becomes detectable and comprehensible over several generations. Charles Darwin, the first to recognize this process, wrote in 1859:

> Owing to this struggle for life, any variation, however slight and from whatever cause proceeding, if it be in any degree profitable to an individual of any species, in its infinitely complex relations to other organic beings and to external nature, will tend to the preservation of that individual, and will generally be inherited by its offspring. The offspring, also, will thus have a better chance of surviving, for, of the many individuals of any species which are periodically born, but a small number can survive. I have called this principle, by which each slight variation, if useful, is preserved, by the term of Natural Selection, in order to mark its relation to man's power of selection. . . . One general law, leading to the advancement of all organic beings, namely, multiply, vary, let the strongest live and the weakest die.[68]

Natural selection requires generations, inheritable traits, variation of the traits, and competition—conditions that are characteristic of all life. All organisms live, reproduce, and die. Their generations range from hours to hundreds of years, but in all cases, their lives follow this pattern. All organisms have offspring with a different mix of inheritable characteristics. Mutations, sex, gene recombination, and gene flow cause these traits to vary among organisms and across generations.

The offspring of all organisms inhabit competitive environments. If territory and resources initially are ample, the organisms proliferate to the point that the territory and resources become in short supply. Once life establishes itself in an area, territories and resources take work to acquire. The offspring that are better able to fulfill their needs and reproduce in the environment continue. They are "naturally selected," and the frequency of their traits increases in the population. This ever-so-slow generational and iterative process evolves all life-forms.

> **Natural Selection** is a natural process that requires inheritable traits, variation of the traits, generations, and competition, where those organisms better suited for their environments place more offspring into the next generation, increasing the frequency of the genes governing the advantageous traits.

As hard as it is to believe, bacteria, algae, fungi, worms, spiders, bananas, frogs, crocodiles, robins, dogs, monkeys, and humans all result from a long series of successive and infinitesimally small changes over large spans of time. The concept of gradualism helps us understand evolution and the process of natural selection.

> **Gradualism** is the reality that a series of imperceptible, small changes accumulate into tremendous, unrecognizable transformations over large spans of time.

Consider the evolution of giraffes from a species similar in nature to the zebra. Some thirty to fifty million years ago, zebra-like animals were numerous on the plains of Africa. Some of these zebra-like animals had slightly longer necks and could graze on the higher vegetation. These animals could feed themselves, survive, and successfully reproduce when the vegetation closer to the ground became in short supply. As these flourishing longer-necked animals mated with one another, more of their longer-neck genes populated this gene pool. As this process occurred iteratively over hundreds of years, a reach advantage of inches became feet.

Giraffes with necks longer than modern giraffes did not do well. Their necks were too long and interfered with daily life. These giraffes did not reproduce as well as their shorter-neck counterparts. In this manner, natural selection lengthened the necks of giraffes to the point where longer necks provided advantage in feeding but not disadvantage in daily living.

The ability of the longer-necked animals to survive and successfully reproduce provides an excellent example of how a series of small changes accumulated into a large one over numerous generations. Amazingly, each form of life has changed and adapted to its environment in a similar manner, but because the process is glacially slow, it is imperceptible to us.

The breeding of animals by humans for hundreds of years is an example of a directed selection process. We can see the handiwork of this iterative selection or "breeding" in dogs. From the Chihuahua to the Great Dane, all the breeds of dogs descend from a common gray wolf ancestor that lived some 130,000 years ago and people's selection of offspring with various desired traits over thousands of years.[69] World renowned Harvard biologist E. O. Wilson writes:

> The theory of population genetics, and experiments on other organisms, show that substantial changes can occur in the span of less than 100 generations, which for man reaches back to the time of the Roman Empire.[70]

The domestic turkey, with which I have years of experience, is now over two hundred generations removed from the wild turkey. By selectively breeding the white-feathered, broader-breasted, faster-growing turkeys, breeders created commercial turkeys very different from the wild turkey in relatively few generations.

The evolution of life and natural selection become clearer to us as we selectively breed plants and animals. Students can observe this process and a species' evolution in shorter maturation species like fruit flies in college biology courses in just a few weeks.

Interrelated Products of the Past

It is a mistake to think that the past is dead. Nothing
that has ever happened is quite without influence at this
moment. The present is merely the past rolled up and con-
centrated in this second of time. You, too, are your past;
often your face is your autobiography; you are what you
are because of what you have been; because of your hered-
ity stretching back into forgotten generations; because of
every element of environment that has affected you, every
man or woman that has met you, every book that you have
read, every experience that you have had; all these are
accumulated in your memory, your body, your character,
your soul. So with a city, a country, and a race; it is its past,
and cannot be understood without it.[71]

—Will and Ariel Durant

The universe is vast and repetitious, but it is also interrelated. It
started from a point in time and space, expanding outward through time.
The universe had a hot beginning. As it cooled, it coalesced into trillions
of galaxies and trillions of trillions of stars, planets, and planetesimal
bodies. Its living stars assemble twenty-six of the elements, and some of
its dying stars the remaining elements. The elements self-assemble into
molecules, and some of the molecules into nucleotides.

Under the right conditions, it appears some of the nucleotides
assembled into RNA, DNA, numerous other amino acids, proteins, and
one or more cells. Then, one or more cells started dividing and replicat-
ing. Under the direction of DNA and the selection pressure of an environment, some of the resulting cells formed multicellular organisms,
and some multicellular organisms formed superorganisms. And just as
the galaxies, stars, planets, planetesimal bodies, elements, and nucleotides occur throughout the universe, I believe that one day we will learn

that RNA, DNA, amino acids, proteins, cells, multicellular organisms, and superorganisms occur throughout the universe.

From every existing cell's architecture and DNA, scientists know that at least one original cell became a reproductive dividing machine. This cell and its progeny outcompeted all other cells, and since its formation, no other cell seems to have formed from scratch and parented life. All the living cells that scientists have examined appear to come from divisions of this first dominant cell. One human body alone is comprised of several trillion cells. Imagine the cell divisions that have occurred from the original dominant cell throughout the last 3.5 billion years to form every bit of life and cell that has ever lived on Earth.

Germ cells, those in ovaries and testes and which start all forms of life, make the interrelatedness of life possible. They are immortal. They do not age. Under the right conditions and with access to the necessary resources, they may divide ad infinitum. It is the somatic cells, the rest of the cells in our bodies, that age and die.

Thus, we share an interrelated past with all life on Earth. We share a common human ancestor with all other people and common ancestors with primates. We share common ancestors with mammals, reptiles, amphibians, insects, fish, and plants. Most amazing of all, it appears that we share basic nucleotide sequences of the first surviving cell with all terrestrial life-forms.

The evolution of the universe and life is wondrous! Science reveals how the universe and life evolve but nothing about why they evolve. Implicit in why is intent, and scientists find no more intent in evolution than in the flow of a river.

The universe and life as we know it are the cards nature deals us. What matters is what we do with these cards—how we advantageously align with the flow; utilize our circumstances and gifts to advance our families, communities, country, and life; and bridge the 13.7-billion-year past and the future.

Evolution—the gradual change of the universe, life, organization, government, culture, or something else over time. In the case of the evolution of life, it involves variation, inheritable traits, generations, comparative advantage, competition, and natural selection, where organisms better suited for their environments place more offspring into the next generation, increasing the frequency of the genes governing the most advantageous traits.

CHAPTER 7

Fitness

To be or not to be?

Shakespeare's character Hamlet, contemplating existence, poses the question of all questions. While humans sometimes ponder this question, most forms of life just want "to be" by nature. Underlying the actions of most every organism, individual, family, organization, enterprise, country, and culture is the instinct "to be." If this were not the case, the beings and entities would "not be," as being is difficult.

Meritocracy

We always have needed territory, water, food, and shelter to survive. Our continuation depends on these things. For most of us, though, our ancestors secured our territory, and now we only need to purchase or rent a small slice of it, contribute to its defense, earn our livelihoods, buy our resources, and pay our taxes. The defense of territory and procurement of resources for many in the West have become so easy that we forget that we require them. We forget that organisms and groups must win a long series of minor and major competitions for them and that we only flourish as we prevent other life-forms from taking our territory and resources. We hold our ground, or we perish. This has been the reality for billions of years, and it will not change in our lifetimes.

As much as some of us would like to live apart from nature, remove ourselves from competition, and avoid the work of being fit, such thinking is fanciful and foolish. Individuals and organizations wither without competition and the winnowing of the fit from the unfit. One world order, a socialist state, monopolies, quotas, price controls, and socialism are futile pursuits. They are corrupting, debilitating, temporary, and contrary to evolution, and they eventually give way to competitive and meritocratic arrangements.

> **Meritocracy** is assigning the fittest, or the ablest and most qualified people, to the available roles and positions within a group regardless of their age, gender, religion, race, or ethnicity.

I will only introduce meritocracy here and note that it is an essential part of fitness in this chapter. A more detailed discussion of it appears in a subsequent book, *The Winning Practices of a Free, Fit, and Prosperous People.*

Procreation

Besides assigning roles and positions meritoriously, fitness requires procreation. It requires organisms to place as many or more offspring into the next generation as their competitors. Most forms of life are programmed to do this. It is in their DNA, and they cannot do otherwise. Humans have choice, and today many couples are choosing to have fewer children and fewer domestic demands. Those having fewer children want compelling careers and express concern about the finite carrying capacity of the earth. Those having several children play out the program that nature gives us.

Unfortunately, there is a downside to having fewer children that most people do not consider. Having fewer than 2.1 children per family on average erodes the vitality of a population and culture. The population shrinks. Its ability to defend itself, its culture, its winning perspectives and practices, and its influence all decline, while the ability of other populations to do these things grows.

> **Procreation** is the tendency for people to mate and parent children. Family sizes of 2.1 children per female maintain a population, and larger ones increase it.

We may think we would be happier without children, choose our career over having children, and think that having children harms the environment, but we need to replace and increase our numbers to maintain our relevance. We do not need to out-procreate every competitor, but we do need to remain competitive through time. Our personal desires and concern for the earth's ecology do not change our need for demographic and cultural fitness.

We may increase our population with immigrants, but immigrants who do not assimilate create minority subcultures and crippling division. They decrease the prevalence of a highly successful population's Winning Perspectives and Practices and their fitness. The U.S., France, Germany, Greece, the United Kingdom, and Sweden currently have these problems.

So how do we maintain relevance but not overpopulate the world; how can we enjoy a high quality of life without degrading the environment? In short, we work with other countries to reduce population growth, just as we work with them to reduce nuclear weapons, and more specifically, we utilize the Winning Practices described in the next book of the *Flourish* Series.

Generally, we do not see the Islamic cultures as being particularly successful, but they are highly successful. Like medieval Christianity, most expressions of Islam are extremely Darwinian. They encourage their practitioners to have large families. We can see this by comparing their teachings with other religions and by examining the growth of Islamic populations over time. Islamic populations have grown from 0 to 1.6 billion people, or 23 percent of the world's population, in just fourteen hundred years. No other religious group has achieved such growth in fourteen hundred years.

Figure 8 compares the U.S., Islamic, and world populations over time. At current growth rates, Islamic populations will grow to 9.5 billion people and almost half of the world's population in one hundred years. Without immigrants, the U.S. population shrinks.[72] With immigrants, the U.S. population grows from 310 to 840 million people and decreases from 5 to 4 percent of the world's population.

Figure 8: Comparison of the U.S., Islamic, and World Populations over Time

	2012 Population in Millions	Percent of Total Population	Percent Annual Growth Rate	Years to Double	Population after 100 Years in Millions	Percent of Total Population
U.S. Population	310	5	1.0	69	840	4
Islamic Population	1,600	23	1.8	38	9,530	46
World Population	7,000	100	1.1	63	20,900	100

Wikipedia, List of Countries by Population, http://en.wikipedia.org/wiki/List_of_countries_by_population,
Wikipedia, List of Countries by Muslim Population, http://en.wikipedia.org/wiki/List_of_countries_by_
Muslim_population, Wikipedia, List of Countries, by Population Growth Rate, http://en.wikipedia.org/wiki/
List_of_countries_by_population_growth_rate

The unstated and underlying aim of most expressions of Islam is population growth. Most adherents are taught to maintain their faith and distinctive dress, disperse throughout the world, have large families, and convert other people to their faith. Most expressions of Islam encourage their members to embed within populations, increase their numbers, and gradually change the ethnic mix, culture, and laws of a country. The real Islamic threat to the non-Islamic world is not terrorism but demographic and cultural in nature.

From an evolutionary perspective, Jewish populations have the meritocracy aspect of fitness right, and Islamic populations have the procreation aspect of it right. Most developed Western populations have both wrong, and more recently China has both right.

Procreation and immigration are part of life, and what the Islamic populations are doing is nothing new. They are just doing it more successfully now than other populations. In the seventeenth and eighteenth centuries, the English and Spanish populations were very Darwinian. They seeded new lands with their people and cultures and nearly annihilated the indigenous populations of North America, Latin America, South America, Australia, and New Zealand. Their Darwinian actions in the eighteenth century set up our dominance in the nineteenth and twentieth centuries. Professor of geography at UCLA and Pulitzer Prize–winning author Jared Diamond indicates that such ruthless dominance has been the norm for thousands of years:

> Twelve thousand years ago, everybody on earth was a hunter-gatherer; now almost all of us are farmers or else are fed by farmers. The spread of farming from those few sites of origin usually did not occur as a result of the hunter-gatherers' elsewhere adopting farming; hunter-gatherers tend to be conservative. . . . Instead, farming spread mainly through farmers' outbreeding hunters, developing more potent technology, and then killing the hunters or driving them off all lands suitable for agriculture.[73]

Those who think we have evolved beyond this Darwinian behavior are sadly mistaken. Such behavior has been the way of all life for millions of years. Our DNA carries instructions for ruthless domination, and whenever territory and resources are scarce, this behavior and self-righteous justifications for it emerge. Thus, we can no more unilaterally decrease our procreative, political, economic, or military power than our nuclear power. Just as we only decrease our nuclear arsenal when our primary competitor, Russia, decreases its arsenal, so we must only decrease our procreation when China, India, Brazil, and the Islamic countries decrease their procreation.

A study of evolution, the universe, and life also suggests that one day we will face competition from extraterrestrial life. This is not certain but likely. The redundancy observed throughout the universe, the predisposition of the universe and life to self-assemble, and the existence of billions of potentially habitable planets suggest that the universe probably is teeming with life. This insight raises a question that I often posed to my management teams over the years: Are we fit enough to withstand the competition from unknown as well as known sources?

Fitter organisms must have the offspring, and the offspring must realize as much of their potential as possible for a population to do well over time. Ironically, as Western countries grow more complex, those who are the least fit for modern life have many children and those who are most fit have few children.

Although our ancestors did not understand evolution, they worked out many advantageous practices to raise fit and well-adjusted children. The practices of postponing sex until marriage, marrying young, having larger families, and lifelong marriage gave us large numbers of well-adjusted, able children.

Contrast these past practices to the current practices of "hooking-up," separating, single parenting, and small family sizes, and one quickly gains a sense of our procreative and child development failures. Where past generations focused more on the next generation, we focus more on ourselves. Birth control, abortion on demand, recreational sex, career-centric fathers and mothers, weak marriage commitments, sexually transmitted disease (STDs), and related infertility all diminish our population's long-term health, development, and viability.

Our culture's current practice of channeling one-third of its public resources to less fit and productive people is also counterproductive. Such misguided policies increase poverty and human suffering over time. Channeling more of these resources into research and development, general fitness, and the colonization of space would enhance our fitness and benefit future generations more. In later chapters, I discuss superior, less costly ways to empower people and reduce poverty.

To be clear, I am not suggesting that we should control our procreation, but I am suggesting that our culture and policies should encourage fit, married people to have children and discourage unmarried people from having children. Although this approach might seem old-fashioned, it aligns with evolution and nature. Moreover, it diminishes human suffering and improves a people's health over time.

Consider the effects of the following six realities, first individually and then collectively. While each reality should concern us, the six realities together are tantamount to cultural suicide and the surrender of all we hold dear. They are a disaster for our great-grandchildren and should cause us to change our ways.

1. At current growth rates, the number of Muslims in the world will increase by several billion in the next one hundred years.

2. Most Muslims have perspectives and practices that are antithetical to traditional Western ones.

3. As the extremist members of these groups attack us, rather than decisively retaliating against the governments who fund them and the mullahs who instruct them, we only pursue those committing the violent acts. Rather than prohibiting the entry of the zealous mullahs and Muslims into our country, we invite them and financially support many of them. Rather than acting to expeditiously end the conflicts and discourage future attacks, we act in a manner that prolongs the conflicts, maims our youth, and drains our treasury.

4. We have children at rates that do not sustain our population and culture.

5. Many of the people who have children are the people least able to raise them.

6. Though our numbers decrease, and Muslim numbers rapidly increase, we expend massive amounts of resources to advance democracy throughout the world.

We do not foresee the cumulative and long-term effects of our policies, programs, and practices. If we did, we would change them.

The Underlying Aim of Life

Thomas Jefferson wrote in The Declaration of Independence:

> We hold these truths to be self-evident, that all [people]
> are created equal, that they are endowed by their creator
> with certain unalienable rights, that among these are life,
> liberty, and the pursuit of happiness.[74]

Somehow, this declaration of people's equality before the law and basic rights now means to many people that life is primarily about the pursuit of happiness. This is so unfortunate, as those who pursue happiness seldom find it. In my experience, the happiest people are those who pursue fitness, or in other words, people who maintain their health, treat others well, apply themselves in school, make their marriage work, parent children well, earn their livelihood, contribute to their communities, and mentor their grandchildren.

Happiness is not the aim of life. Fitness is the aim of life, and fitness is what brings happiness. It is its own reward. Fitness brings us health, competence, and affiliation with other able people. It brings us the esteem of others, desirable mates, and long life. It brings us offspring and the continuation of our culture and institutions.

Evolution delineates our end and circumscribes our means. It gives us some latitude to be foolish in the short term but not the long term. It reveals that fitness is our end, and unilaterally shrinking our population or disarming assures irrelevance and extinction. The sooner we make fitness our individual, familial, and collective goal, the sooner we will rediscover our way, enjoy greater success, and find greater happiness.

Fitness—the ability of organisms to flourish, procure needed resources, and reproduce relative to other organisms. Fitness is the underlying aim of life and its own reward.

CHAPTER 8

Human Nature

We avoid pain and pursue pleasure. We compete for resources, mates, and influence. We pursue our self-interest and children's interests first, our affiliated interests second, and others' interests third. These inclinations work on us twenty-four hours a day, seven days a week.

Scientists have persuasively demonstrated that genes direct the development of our bodies and our inclinations. Genes nudge us to engage in numerous behaviors that aid survival and perpetuate our DNA. If this were not the case, we would gradually exit the evolutionary stage.

The consistent way in which our genes drive our inclinations results in common tendencies that we call human nature. Charles Darwin and Abraham Maslow did an excellent job characterizing human nature and identifying a hierarchy of human needs. My thoughts build on their insights.

Individual and Familial

Fundamental to all life is an inclination to seek pleasure and avoid pain. This is a life-preserving inclination. We eat food and drink water because they sustain us, alleviate pain, and bring pleasure. We procure clothing, shelter, and security because they protect us, comfort us, and alleviate pain. These tendencies are obvious and self-evident. We would not live long without them.

Other tendencies are psychological, less obvious, and often culturally shaped. We work to earn money to purchase the things that bring us pleasure and help us avoid pain. We work to obtain the esteem of others and for social acceptance. We tell the truth to gain our parents' approval and avoid their anger. In the last two examples, the pleasure sought, and the pain avoided, are not physical but psychological. They are shaped by our genes, families, cultures, and environments.

We have strong inclinations to understand the world, develop, and actualize. We see these tendencies in our children. We devote large portions of our time and resources to learning and developing skills. We attend school for thirteen or more years and spend weeks, months, and years learning our jobs. We also want to play on the stage. If we have musical ability, we make beautiful music. If we have artistic talent, we create beautiful art. If we have athletic ability, we compete in athletic competitions. If we have leadership ability, we lead. We develop and deploy the predilections that we inherit and that others encourage.

We are self-centered creatures, especially when we are young. Life is about us. When we are parents, life is largely about our children and us. When we are grandparents, life is about our children, grandchildren, and us. We focus on ourselves and our progeny much more than on others. Self-centered tendencies diminish as we age and as our parents, schools, workplaces, and culture teach us to care about others.

Because we evolved primarily at a time when there was more benefit to short-term thinking than to long-term thinking, we are short-term oriented. We respond to short-term rewards more than to long-term ones. Our short-term tendencies are most apparent in infants and young children. Infants and young children are impatient. Without strong cultural conditioning to learn to defer gratification, these inclinations do not end in childhood. Adults who do not learn to defer gratification buy many things with credit rather than with cash. Their inability to wait lowers their living standards significantly.

Our short-term orientation comes not only from a natural impatience but also from a tendency to overweight what is freshest in our minds. Recent memories dominate longer-term ones. For example, after a series of misfortunes, we become pessimistic. After a run of good fortune, we become overconfident. We want to invest in the assets that did well last year even though they cost more and avoid assets that declined in value though they cost less and are more likely to appreciate.

Our short-term tendencies make many of the activities that lead to success in modern life difficult for us. They make studiousness, frugality, perseverance, and accomplishment difficult. They make rising after several defeats and exercising good judgment after several successes difficult.

Most of us also prefer small, certain rewards to larger, uncertain ones. Our aversion to losses makes entrepreneurship and investing unappealing to most people, and it is a primary reason why entrepreneurs and investors need opportunities to profit. Without opportunities to profit, people are too risk-averse to start businesses, save, invest, and undertake many of the other activities that improve our lives.

We also have a strong desire to create homes and reside in aesthetically pleasing places. Homes are comfortable refuges, opportunities to actualize, and statements of social status. We spend many of our resources and much of our discretionary time procuring and shaping our homes.

Along with our individual nature, we have a strong familial nature. We want to love, be loved, procreate, and see our children and grandchildren flourish. If this were not the case, our species would not be doing well. Familial tendencies are so strong that they dominate adult motivation.

Social

Along with our individual and familial natures, we have a social nature. At some point in our past, our ancestors found living in groups advantageous. In groups, they could better defend themselves. They could more easily build homes, grow food, kill five-ton mastodons, and clothe themselves. E. O. Wilson observes:

> The only other mammalian carnivores that take outsized prey are lions, hyenas, wolves, and African wild dogs. Each of these species has an exceptionally advanced social life, prominently featuring the pursuit of prey in coordinated packs. . . . Primitive [humans] are ecological analogs of lions, wolves, and hyenas. . . . And they resemble four-footed carnivores more than other primates by habitually slaughtering surplus prey, storing food, feeding solid food to their young, dividing labor, practicing cannibalism, and

interacting aggressively with competing species. Bones and stone tools dug from ancient campsites in Africa, Europe, and Asia indicate that this way of life persisted for a million years or longer and was abandoned in most societies only during the last few thousands of years.[75]

Scientists consider organisms that ally with others to be "superorganisms." Superorganism affiliation conveys fitness—the strength found in numbers, economies of scale, and opportunities to specialize, trade, and synergize.

> A **Superorganism** is a subpopulation of a species bound together genetically, biologically, and sometimes culturally that functions and competes as a unit.

Ants form colonies; bees, hives; wolves, packs; lions, prides; gorillas, troops; and humans—families, clans, tribes, cities, states, and countries. Humans also form clubs, associations, enterprises, universities, international alliances, and countless other organizations, and they belong to numerous superorganisms simultaneously.

Eons of natural selection have honed our social and superorganism nature, and thus, it serves our self-interest. We not only seek money to procure products and services that bring us pleasure, but we also seek it for the social status and influence it brings. We seek power and influence within groups to secure our standing and to affect their agendas.

Surprising to most people but less so to students of evolution, even altruism serves our self-interest. Altruism is not just selfless concern for others. Rather, it generally is some self-interest wrapped in a concern for others. Altruism advances our standing within groups and increases the likelihood of receiving aid from them. Journalist, scholar, and award-winning author Robert Wright describes this in his landmark work, *The Moral Animal:*

Altruism, compassion, empathy, love, conscience, the sense of justice—all these things, the things that hold society together, the things that allow our species to think so highly of itself, can now confidently be said to have a firm genetic basis. That's the good news. The bad news is that, although these things are in some ways blessings for humanity, they didn't evolve for the "good of the species" and aren't reliably employed to that end. Quite the contrary: it is now clearer than ever how (and precisely why) the moral sentiments are used with brutal flexibility, switched on and off in keeping with self-interest; and how naturally oblivious we often are to this switching. In the new view, human beings are a species splendid in their array of moral equipment, tragic in their propensity to misuse it, and pathetic in their constitutional ignorance of the misuse.[76]

Although the unselfish aspects of our nature ultimately serve our self-interest, we should not despair or become cynical. Altruism, compassion, empathy, love, conscience, and justice are essential to group function, and affiliation only conveys fitness as we exhibit these characteristics and work together. Too much individualism and separation erode the benefits of affiliation: strength of numbers, economies of scale, and opportunities to specialize, trade, and synergize.

One final note on our social nature is that we have a very strong natural tendency to absorb the thinking of our groups and disregard information that challenges it. This tendency furthers affiliation and our opportunity to reap its benefits. It increases our ability to work with others and strengthens groups. And most of the time, we are not even aware of this tendency. It completely eludes us when we are inside a group but is apparent when we are on the outside looking in.

Once we understand our superorganism and social nature and its importance, we realize that (a) the individual is not preeminent, (b) we have individual, familial, and social natures, (c) we must balance the requisites of these natures, and (d) sometimes individuals must sacrifice themselves for their larger groups.

Environmental Alignment

As long as we inhabited environments like the hunter-gatherer environments from which we evolved, our genes did an excellent job of driving our behaviors. This is because, as E. O. Wilson notes:

> The selection pressures of hunter-gatherer existence have persisted for over 99 percent of human evolution.[77]

Different environments favor, or select for, different organism characteristics. The savannahs and forests of the hunter-gatherer were no different. They favored relatively small, mobile groups, or tribes, comprised of individuals who worked together cooperatively to defend themselves and secure scarce nutrients.

When our environments become significantly different from the hunter-gatherer environments and/or we confront foreign substances, some of our hunter-gatherer genetic tendencies adversely affect us. Environmental pressures require generations to shape our genetic inclinations. When our environment changes in just a few generations, as has been the case in the last 150 years, we must consciously direct our behaviors more and override some of our genetic inclinations. Intelligence, leadership, enculturation, and discipline further our success in rapidly changing environments.

Tobacco, alcohol, drugs, caffeine, sweets, fats, salt, and pornography were not readily available throughout most of our evolutionary history. Natural selection has not populated the gene pool with genomes that incline us to avoid these things. Thus, these pleasure-titillating substances and activities pose serious challenges to us. Once they pleasure our brains, we want more of them, even though we know they can be addictive and harmful.

If we are fortunate, our parents, teachers, coaches, and mentors condition us to avoid many harmful behaviors and substances. If we are not so fortunate, we must develop an aversion to them ourselves.

Because it is tough for people to counter human nature on their own, we want to create laws, policies, institutions, and environments to mitigate these challenges as much as possible. Getting people to overcome the genetic inclinations that act upon them twenty-four hours a day, seven days a week takes concerted effort.

If we want to improve our families and institutions, we must utilize practices developed with an understanding of human nature. Ignorance of human nature and attempts to improve the world have serious unintended consequences. David Brooks writes:

> I believe we inherit a great river of knowledge, a flow of patterns coming from many sources. The information that comes from deep in the evolutionary past we call genetics. The information passed along from hundreds of years ago we call culture. The information passed along from decades ago we call family, and the information offered months ago we call education. But it is all information that flows through us. The brain is adapted to the river of knowledge and exists only as a creature in that river. Our thoughts are profoundly molded by this long historic flow, and none of us exists, self-made, in isolation from it.[78]

The genius of a prudently regulated free enterprise and free market, when they are tempered by common ethics, sound laws, and an effective justice system, is that they work with human nature, encouraging people to pursue their self-interest in ways that benefit the larger superorganism. The entrepreneurs and employees who work hard to make their living and a profit improve the affordability and desirability of products and services.

Unlike free enterprise, socialism does not harness people's self-interest, and socialistic, non-meritocratic groups eventually find themselves at the mercy of freer, meritocratic ones. People's rewards must vary with the risks they take and their quality and quantity of work. People cannot be demeaned and ostracized for taking risks, working hard, and doing well, as they frequently are in socialistic arrangements.

Free enterprise sometimes offends our sense of fairness, but competitive forms of it improve our living standards. Socialism appeals to our sense of fairness but diminishes its adherents' living standards. I describe a stakeholder inclusion and Goldilocks minimum wage arrangements that make free enterprise fairer in ways that avoid the unintended, adverse consequences of socialism in *The Winning Practices of a Free, Fit, and Prosperous People.*

Usually, unions are unfortunate responses to neglectful and/or abusive management. Like socialism, they appeal to people's sense of fairness, but they also carry several adverse, unintended consequences. Generally, unions do not affect who manages a business, but they do change the work rules and temper management abusiveness. They limit management's discretion, create inefficiencies, and divide management and labor in organizations. They force managers to reward seniority at the expense of merit, and in doing so, they further mediocrity.

Those who promote unions do so with the good-hearted intentions of protecting employees and raising middle-class wages and benefits. While unions protect their employees and improve their wages and benefits in the short term, they also make enterprises less competitive and frequently cause members to lose their jobs in the long term. Unions raise the prices of products and services and lower non-member living standards. Those who more critically consider the effects of unions realize that consumer losses and the eventual loss of employees' jobs, related economic activity, and related tax revenue more than offset members' short-term gains.

Human nature is one of the cards nature deals us. It is not something that we can change in our lifetimes. Winning practices harness human nature and stream positive effects. Losing practices ignore human nature and stream unintended negative effects. Understanding human nature and aligning our policies, organizations, and practices with it improve our fitness and well-being dramatically.

Human Nature—*a collection of universal individual, familial, and social tendencies that include (a) avoiding pain and pursuing pleasure, (b) seeking water, food, clothing, shelter, security, and others' esteem, (c) understanding the world, developing, and actualizing, (d) seeking money, power, and influence, (e) loving, being loved, and procreating, (f) doing the best by one's children, (g) having a short-term orientation, (h) having an aversion to losses, (i) securing aesthetically pleasing environments, (j) affiliating with others in mutually beneficial ways, (k) absorbing others' thinking, and pursuing one's interests first, the interests of those with whom we affiliate second, and the interests of others last.*

CHAPTER 9

Periodic Disaster

*Life is not without its challenges or for the faint of heart. The universe
and planet are violent and perilous places.*

The earth's fossil record indicates that more than half of all living species became extinct during five catastrophic periods, occurring
approximately 70, 200, 250, 380, and 450 million years ago.[79] Mass
extinctions occur infrequently but dramatically change the mix of life
on earth when they do. Scientists are not sure of the causes of these
mass extinctions, but they hypothesize that supernova explosions, solar
eruptions, asteroid impacts, planetary polarization changes, volcanic
eruptions, and platonic shifts sometimes alter climate and sea levels
enough to cause them. These five catastrophic extinctions warn us that
conditions can change drastically on earth.

Along with dramatic climate changes, diseases and famines have
devastated populations throughout history. Virulent viruses and bacteria reduced some European populations by more than 50 percent in the
seventh and fourteenth centuries.[80] Famines accelerated the decline of
the Egyptian, Roman, Mayan, and Byzantine empires.[81]

Historians estimate that famines reduced the populations of Central America (800–1000), France (1693–94), Iran (1870–71), Ireland
(1845–49), Indonesia (1944–45), Cambodia (1975–79), and the Congo
(1998–2004) by more than one million people. The former Soviet
Union lost millions of people to famine during four periods—1916–17,
1932–33, 1941–44, and 1947—in the last one hundred years. China lost
forty-five million people during the 1810, 1811, 1846, and 1849 famines,
sixty million people during the 1850–73 famine, another twenty-five
million people during the 1907–11 famine, and millions more during
the 1928–30, 1936, and 1959–61 famines. India lost millions of people
during nine major famines occurring between 1700 and 1950.[82]

War also has reduced populations throughout history. Figure 9 lists the major wars and conflicts with more than one-quarter of a million casualties. The figure suggests that the world is seldom free of war, and it should give people who maintain that we have evolved to the point where we no longer need a strong defense reason to reconsider this position.

The planetary record and history indicate that life must endure and overcome many hardships. They suggest that we would be wise to prepare for epidemics, famines, wars, and challenging times; to learn to deflect asteroids from earth; and to develop technology to colonize space. Carl Sagan wrote:

> Since, in the long run, every planetary society will be endangered by impacts from space, every surviving civilization is obliged to become spacefaring—not because of exploratory or romantic zeal, but for the most practical reason imaginable: staying alive.[83]

We live in a rough neighborhood. The universe and earth are dangerous places. It appears that we are on our own. Our continuation depends on numbers, fitness, preparation, healthy planetary habitats, and our eventual dispersion throughout our galaxy.

Periodic Disaster—the reality that our universe and planet are dangerous places. Earthquakes, typhoons, tsunamis, tornados, wildfires, floods, famines, disease, and war regularly erode our populations. Quasars, supernovas, solar eruptions, asteroid impacts, planetary polarization changes, volcanic eruptions, and major platonic shifts periodically trigger significant climate and sea level changes that devastate or even eliminate many forms of life.

Figure 9: Major Wars and Conflicts
with Greater than 250,000 Casualities

Second Punic War	218—201 BC
Gallic Wars	58—50 BC
Three Kingdoms War	184—280
An Lushan Rebellion	755—763
Muslim Conquests on the Indian Subcontinent	1100—1600
Mongol Conquests	1206—1324
Conquests of Tamur	1370—1405
Conquest of Mehmed II the Conqueror	1451—1481
Conquests of the Americas	1492—1691
French Wars of Religion	1562—1598
Japanese Invasions of Korea	1592—1598
Qing Conquest of Ming Dynasty	1616—1662
Thirty Years War	1618—1648
Wars of the Three Kingdoms	1639—1651
English Civil War	1642—1651
Great Northern War	1700—1721
War of the Spanish Succession	1701—1714
Seven Years War	1756—1763
Napoleonic Wars	1803—1815
Shaku's Conquests	1816—1828
Taiping Rebellion	1850—1864
Crimean War	1853—1856
American Civil War	1861—1865

Dugan Revolt	1862—1877
War of the Triple Alliance	1864—1870
Mexican Revolution	1910—1920
World War I	1914—1918
Russian Civil War and Foreign Intervention	1917—1922
Chinese Civil War	1927—1949
Spanish Civil War	1936—1939
Second Sino-Japanese War	1937—1945
World War II	1939—1945
First Indochina War	1946—1954
Korean War	1950—1953
Algerian War of Independence	1954—1962
Vietnam War/Second Indochina War	1955—1975
Biafra War	1967—1970
Bangladesh Liberation War	1971
Ethiopian Civil War	1974—1991
Soviet War in Afghanistan	1979—1989
Iran-Iraq War/First Persian Gulf War	1980—1988
Somali Civil War	1986—Present
Civil War of Afghanistan	1989—1992
Second Burundian Civil War	1993—2005
War on Terror	2001—Present
Syrian Civil War	2007—Present

List of Wars by Death Toll, Wikipedia,
https://en.wikipedia.org/wiki/List_of_wars_by_death_toll

CHAPTER 10

Eco-Dependency

Our prowess and procreation serve us well until we deplete needed resources or irrevocably harm our planetary ecosystems.

We and all life need natural habitats. Natural habitats do many things for us, and they do them at a lower cost than our best engineers. They provide fresh oxygenated air to breathe, clean water to drink, and fertile soil to grow food.

Wetlands and floodplains filter water and reduce flooding. Topsoil, earthworms, and bacteria provide us with a medium to grow food and a means to decompose waste. Farmlands, grasslands, and forests filter water and convert carbon dioxide to oxygen. They provide us with animal feed, food, wood pulp, and timber. Mangroves, coral reefs, oyster reefs, and seagrass beds filter water and protect coastlines. They provide us with fish and seafood. Eco-dependency is the reality that we depend on natural habitats for clean air and water, food, and a hospitable climate.

Rachel Carson made many people aware of our negative impacts on natural habitats with her publication of *Silent Spring* in 1962. Scientists have inventoried these impacts since, and large portions of our population have learned about their findings. We have learned that we drained and developed millions of acres of wetlands and floodplains; contaminated our groundwater, streams, rivers, and lakes with fertilizers, petroleum products, sewage, road salt, pesticides, herbicides, hormones, and other harmful substances; destroyed thousands of miles of mangroves, coral reefs, and oyster reefs; and dumped millions of tons of trash into the seas.

We have learned that we have cleared millions of acres of forests and grasslands; significantly raised carbon dioxide levels in our atmosphere; contaminated our atmosphere with carbon monoxide, nitrous oxide, sulfur dioxide, lead, and other particulates; scuttled ships with radioactive reactors; and stored underground approximately 74,000 tons of highly radioactive waste, which must remain sealed for tens of thousands of years.[84]

Each year we destroy a few hundred of the estimated two million species, even though we depend on so many species and habitats directly and indirectly. Species destruction is irreversible, and it affects critical ecosystems, which in turn affect earth's climate. E. O. Wilson writes:

> The worst thing that can happen during the [near term] is not energy depletion, economic collapse, limited nuclear war, or conquest by a totalitarian government. As terrible as these disasters would be for us, they can be repaired within a few generations. The one process ongoing in the [near term] that will take millions of years to correct is the loss of genetic and species diversity by the destruction of natural habitats. This is the folly that our descendants are least likely to forgive us.[85]

We cannot and should not attempt to preserve every species at all costs. Our resources are finite, and the extinction of an unfit species is a natural part of evolution. However, we can reduce our environmental footprint, protect as many species as practically possible, and save the species that are critical to our ecosystems.

Asteroid impacts, polarization changes, volcanic eruptions, and other extraterrestrial shocks can dramatically change the earth's climate, and now it seems that humans can as well. Scientists persuasively demonstrate that carbon dioxide (CO_2), methane (CH_4), nitrous oxide (N_2O), and other greenhouse gases trap solar energy within the atmosphere and increase planetary temperatures. They estimate that postindustrial human activity adds some thirty billion metric tons of CO_2 to the atmosphere each year.[86] It is in our interests to reduce our greenhouse gas emissions.

Although the specific predictions of temperature, rainfall, and sea level changes associated with various human activities and the best ways to mitigate the negative impacts are controversial, most well-informed people agree that we are seriously harming the flora, fauna, and natural habitats on which we depend; we must mitigate our negative impacts on the environment as much as practically possible, and we must slow the world's population growth.

Undoubtedly, enough of a change in the concentration of CO_2 and other greenhouse gases in the atmosphere will change the earth's temperatures and climate. Common sense alone suggests that photosynthesis (CO_2 depletion) must balance with respiration and fossil fuel use (CO_2 emission) in the long term for the climate to remain stable. Our tremendous emission of greenhouse gases and deforestation of thousands of acres every year are unsustainable and climate altering.

Greenhouse gas emissions and deforestation represent externalities that governments must incentivize us to curb. What are externalities?

> **Externalities** are situations where one party's actions create a cost or a benefit to another party who did not choose to bear the cost or receive the benefit. CO_2 emissions and deforestation are examples of externalities. The public, rather than the carbon users and landholders, bear many of the undesirable ancillary effects of these activities in the form of sickness, disease, shortened lifespans, and climate change.

One of the best ways to address undesirable externalities is for governments to tax them and incentivize individuals, enterprises, and other organizations to reduce their emissions. If the government taxed CO_2 emissions, emitters would raise the prices of their products to recoup the tax in the short term and develop more carbon neutral forms of energy in the long term. In response to the higher prices, customers of large CO_2 emitters would purchase less of their products and decrease CO_2 emissions in the short term.

Taxing externalities is one of the best ways to reduce them because a tax does not narrowly address the problem, enlarge the bureaucracy, or micromanage their reduction. Taxing externalities penalizes the undesirable activity and, in doing so, incentivizes everyone to creatively find ways to curtail the undesirable activity.

Finally, we must protect our ecosystems all over the planet. We may procure our oxygen, water, and nutrients locally, but ecosystems on the other side of the planet affect us. We must clean up our activities at home and work with other countries to clean up their activities abroad. Heavy CO_2 emission in North America and Asia, deforestation in South America, and desertification in North Africa affect everyone.

Our lives and future depend on our ecosystems. We must take commonsense steps to stop harming them. Human activity is now sufficient to irreparably turn our beautiful life-giving planet into a desolate one. Carl Sagan writes:

> A tiny blue dot set in a sunbeam. Here it is. That's where we live. That's home. We humans are one species, and this is our world. It is our responsibility to cherish it. Of all the worlds in our solar system, the only one so far as we know, graced by life.[87]

Eco-Dependency—*the reality that the earth's ecosystems sustain us, and the reality that we must minimize our impact on them, protect other species as much as possible, use sustainable agricultural practices that protect groundwater and preserve topsoil, stop the destruction of savannahs and forests, and help plants and animals repair the damaged ecosystems. Eco-Dependency compels us to develop environmentally friendly alternatives to harmful biological, chemical, and nuclear agents, responsibly dispose of the existing ones, recycle our waste, maintain friendly carbon-dioxide-to-oxygen ratios, use carbon-neutral forms of energy, and work with other countries to reduce the world's population growth.*

Winning Perspectives Summary

The Winning Perspectives indicate that we are perceptive, thinking beings who must both proactively and prudently look out for ourselves.

Truth, *like an accurate roadmap, enables us to grasp reality, trust one another, and work together. Our initial perceptions are only a start on our quest for truth. We must read, travel, verify what others tell us, solicit different views, conduct experiments, and gather evidence. Increasing numbers of varied perspectives and amounts of evidence improves our perceptions. They make us more intelligent and our solutions iteratively more effective.*

Causality *assures us that one or more causes underlie every event and that there exists a recipe for everything that happens. The invisible and delayed nature of many causal relationships blinds us to the effects of many of our actions. Mentors, experts, science, and experience expose the effects of our actions and help us act more prudently.*

Scale *reveals the enormity of the universe and the minuteness of its building blocks. It provides us with a realistic view of the universe, its workings, and our place in it. We learn that we live in one of more than a trillion galaxies, orbit around one of the over one billion stars in our galaxy, and live on one of the billions of potentially hospitable planets in the universe. We realize that all earth life-forms descend from a common life-form, we are the products of over three billion years of natural selection, and we may become a fallen leaf from the evolutionary tree or a branch to hundreds, thousands, or even millions of generations of life.*

Evolution *is the ultimate continuous improvement story. It involves variation, inheritable traits, generations, comparative advantage, competition, and natural selection, where organisms better suited for their environments place more offspring into the next generation, increasing the frequency of the genes governing the most advantageous traits. Evolution reveals that fitness is our end, fitness enables us to persist through time, and competitions and comparative advantage play important roles in our lives. Competitions drive evolution. They winnow the disadvantageous from the advantageous. They* decide who wins and allocate positions and resources to those who most ably use them. Comparative advantage assures there exists a role for everyone in a community.

Fitness—or the ability of organisms to flourish, procure needed resources, and reproduce relative to other organisms—requires competence, meritocracy, and procreation. Fitness furthers health, performance, and affiliation. It brings the esteem of others, desirable mates, offspring, and lifelong well-being. It enables our families, institutions, communities, country, and culture to persist through time.

Human Nature is a collection of universal individual, familial, and social tendencies that include (a) avoiding pain and pursuing pleasure, (b) seeking water, food, clothing, shelter, security, and others' esteem, (c) understanding the world, developing, and actualizing, (d) seeking money, power, and influence, (e) loving, being loved, and procreating, (f) doing our best by our children, (g) having a short-term orientation, (h) having an aversion to losses, (i) securing aesthetically pleasing environments, (j) affiliating with others in mutually beneficial ways, (k) absorbing others' thinking, and (l) pursuing one's interests first, the interests of those with whom we affiliate second, and the interests of others last.

Periodic Disaster is the reality that our universe and planet are dangerous places and that our continuation depends on our ability to survive catastrophes, diseases, famines, and wars. Earthquakes, typhoons, tsunamis, tornados, wildfires, floods, famines, disease, and war regularly erode our populations. Quasars, supernovas, solar eruptions, asteroid impacts, planetary polarization changes, volcanic eruptions, and major platonic shifts may periodically trigger significant climate and sea level changes that eliminate many forms of life. Our continuation depends on numbers, fitness, preparation, healthy planetary habitats, and our eventual dispersion throughout our galaxy.

Eco-Dependency is the reality that the earth's ecosystems sustain us, and we must (a) minimize our impact on them, (b) protect other species as much as possible, (c) use sustainable agricultural practices that protect groundwater and preserve topsoil, (d) stop the destruction of savannahs *and forests, (e) help plants and animals repair the damaged ecosystems, (f) develop environmentally friendly alternatives to harmful biological, chemical, and nuclear agents and responsibly dispose of the existing ones, (g) recycle our waste, (h) maintain friendly carbon-dioxide-to-oxygen ratios, (i) use carbon-neutral forms of energy, and (j) work with other countries to reduce the world's population growth.*

Winning Perspectives help us distinguish Winning Practices and improve our effectiveness, fitness, and well-being. They have helped me immensely throughout my life. I am confident that they will help you.

CHAPTER 11

Winning Practices

Because we find strength in numbers, economies of scale, efficiencies in specialization, and synergy in working together, we depend on multiple levels of human organization. We can do everything right as individuals but still have a miserable life if our culture perpetuates dysfunction at the other levels.

Human life is complex. We live and act on many levels. We are born into families, develop into individuals, and form families of our own. We attend school, obtain work, affiliate with many groups, and reside in a country. An individual, familial, and social tri-nature permeates and shapes our lives.

A lot must go right for us to flourish. We need a healthy set of genes, able parents, good schools, profitable employment, functional governments, and helpful cultural norms. When thinking about the practices that are necessary for our fitness and well-being, I had the benefit of the Winning Perspectives and thought about several levels of human organization: individual, family, group, education, enterprise, government, and culture.

Individual

The individual level of human life is particularly important, as we are first and foremost individuals, and the effectiveness of the other levels depends on the fitness of the individuals who constitute them. Millions of years of natural selection hardwired many tendencies into us that act unconsciously on us twenty-four hours a day, seven days a week. These tendencies incline us to pursue our individual and family interests first, the interests of those with whom we affiliate second, and others' interests third. We must consider this in all other levels of human organization. Failure to recognize and harness these tendencies is the primary cause of unintended consequences and organizational ineffectiveness.

Family

Our parents shape us before we shape ourselves. They pass many of their genes to us and teach us innumerable perspectives and practices. They influence who we become and what we do more than others. Families do for children what no other level of human organization does for them.

Human maturation is a tremendous amount of work. Parents must provide love, discipline, perspective, instruction, resources, and opportunities to their children for years. Other role models, mentors, and schools help parents with this responsibility. Loving children and teaching them self-control, to defer gratification, to persevere, and to be open to new perspectives and experiences helps them do well in school and in life.

Groups

Individuals also belong to numerous groups. These groups may be educational, professional, social, recreational, religious, or political in nature. In groups, we learn, play, earn our livelihoods, provide and receive services, socialize, and further common objectives. Often taken for granted, groups enhance our fitness and well-being. They provide us with protection and opportunities to learn from and socialize with others. They allow us to specialize, realize economies of scale, and synergize. They offer us opportunities to develop leadership and team skills. They enable us to aid those in need.

Education

Education enables us to acquire the knowledge and skills that we need to provide for ourselves, successfully raise a family, and contribute to the larger community. It gives us access to the immense reservoir of perspectives and knowledge accumulated by others over time. Education supplements our instincts. It is more important today than ever before because life is so complex. Foods, fabrics, materials, homes, appliances, cars, phones, and medical services are so much more technical than those of just one hundred years ago. Larger communities and populations, science, and technology, microprocessors, the Internet, and artificial intelligence further increase the complexity of our environment, work, products, and lives.

Schools, the primary agents of education, enable children to play, learn, and interact with others. Effective schools teach children (a) basic reading, writing, speaking, and math skills, (b) the scientific method and science's findings regarding the evolution of the universe, earth, and life, (c) our multicultural heritage, (d) a sense of history, and (e) career skills. Effective schools familiarize children with our knowledge base, provide children able role models and mentors, and help children to form enabling habits and avoid debilitating ones.

Children enjoy a smorgasbord of activities in good schools. They experience different types of art and music. They learn to speak foreign languages, to be physically fit, and to win and lose gracefully. They learn about free enterprise, free markets, good government, the real world, and what works.

Enterprise

Efficient, competitive, and stakeholder-oriented enterprises create needed and affordable products and services. They enable us to earn our livelihoods, support our families, and contribute to our communities. These enterprises supply affordable, high-quality housing and related services. They enable one in 400 people to provide our population with inexpensive, high-quality food products, and they indirectly fund our defense, education, healthcare, research, government, social safety net, and retirement. They make possible unprecedented amounts of free time.

Efficient, competitive, and stakeholder-oriented enterprises provide safe and desirable work environments. They compensate their employees well, offer superior benefits, and provide opportunities to advance. Some of these enterprises provide computers, communication devices, and Internet access. Many eliminate repetitive, menial jobs. Many improve productivity and steadily raise our living standards. Some enterprises export products and services, decreasing the relative cost of imports.

Government

Government is one of the most consequential levels of human organization. Its effect on its citizens can range from extremely positive to extremely negative. When governments are well conceived, and their leaders are honest and competent, they liberate and empower their citizens. When government leaders are corrupt and incompetent, they harm their populations, sometimes for generations.

Unfortunately, far more examples of corrupt and incompetent governments exist throughout history than honorable and competent ones. One need only to study life during the last four thousand years or to learn about life in Chad, Nigeria, Somalia, Sudan, Zimbabwe, Afghanistan, Syria, Yemen, North Korea, Laos, and Haiti today to recognize the preciousness of honorable and competent governments. Australia, Norway, New Zealand, Singapore, and Switzerland represent some of the governments that do the best by their citizens today.

Culture

Some of the latest science suggests that among other things, humans are a cacophony of genetic and learned algorithms. What are algorithms? Algorithms are a series of steps or recipes. A recipe to make a cake is an algorithm.

The latest science also indicates that the human brain is a series of layered neuro networks of over 100 billion nerve cells, each having some 10,000 connections. When we do something, various groups of neurons fire, and neurons that "fire together wire together." When we do an activity enough times, the firing pattern hardens. We no longer must consciously think about what we are doing. Our brains automate our performance of the activity.

Most adults play out some 95 percent of their days on autopilot, selecting and then playing one algorithm or routine after another. Genes hardwire into us many algorithms or instincts that have aided human survival in the past. These routines are obvious in infants. Then, all our lives we learn thousands of algorithms. Tying our shoes, restraining our emotional outbursts, eating dessert at the end of our meal, and looking for opportunity in difficulties are all examples of commonly learned algorithms.

From this perspective, it becomes obvious that the algorithms that parents, teachers, coaches, mentors, and peers convey to us and how we spend our time affects our brains, fitness, and well-being. While we need a habitable planet, territory, resources, a family, a home, a workplace, and friends to flourish, we also need an empowering operating system, culture, or collection of perspectives and practices to flourish. Evolution and our genes give us an instinctual operating system, and our environment layers on a cultural one.

Culture is human software that orchestrates group activity. It helps us with our roles as children, students, spouses, employees, parents, grandparents, and citizens. It helps us with discipline, conflict resolution, spouse selection, and aging. It assists us with the admittance of people into groups, the assessment of their standing within them, and the removal of people from the groups. It assists us with the universal challenges of leadership, defense, the ownership and use of property, and the procurement and division of resources.[88]

> **Culture** is the perspectives, practices, and taboos that parents, teachers, and others transmit to us, and the art, heroes, and achievements that groups celebrate to reinforce the transmission

Culture works because our genes incline us to affiliate with others, seek others' esteem, and avoid loneliness, disapproval, and ridicule. We feel pride when we please those within our social circles and shame when we disappoint them. We want to be good as opposed to bad members of groups, where good involves loyalty and service to the group and bad involves disloyalty or harm to the group.[89]

Affiliation divides people into "we(s)" and "they(s)." We are comfortable with those in our groups who are like us, and uncomfortable with those outside our groups who are unlike us. We treat insiders more favorably than outsiders. We give freely to insiders and even sacrifice ourselves for them. We are suspicious of outsiders and may even demonize, plunder, or harm them.

Common cultural norms form around history, relatedness, gender, age, physical appearance, dialect, education, profession, living standard, political affiliation, ethnicity, language, and religion. What groups deem acceptable and unacceptable, or laudable and shameful, circumscribes our behavior. Group norms affect what we do, what we do not do, and what we become over time. Every culture is the product of an incredibly large number of its members' perspectives, beliefs, and practices.

Families, schools, workplaces, religions, and more recently, producers of movies and television shows are the greatest transmitters of culture. They pass their perspectives, beliefs, and practices to us. Heroes play a major role in sustaining and transmitting culture. The people we celebrate and shun signal the acceptableness of various behaviors and activities. Our parents, older siblings, teachers, mythical figures, famous leaders, athletes, musicians, and actors comprise many of our heroes.

The culture of our country affects us tremendously. Countries are our modern-day tribes and constitute our largest groups. A study of large groups and countries reveals cyclical patterns of division and merger. Divisions occur when groups split in two, and mergers occur when groups unite. In the past, divisions typically took place when two leaders, each with the support of a viable portion of a tribe, went their separate ways. Mergers occurred as the men of one tribe killed the men of another and integrated the women into their tribe. In both cases, leaders drove the divisions and mergers. Variation in leadership strength and tribal cohesiveness precipitated the divisions and the mergers.

Today, corporations exhibit slightly more civil forms of divisions and mergers. Their divisions and mergers adhere to a legal process. This is not the case with countries. Although rare, their divisions and mergers are both civil and violent. When collections of disparate people aggregate into a country, and its leaders misuse their power, the country may break up, as did the former Soviet Union and some of the Eastern European countries at the end of the twentieth century. These were relatively civil separations. The recent breakup of the Ukraine provides an example of a violent separation. Sometimes divided peoples merge. This happened relatively recently with East and West Germany and might one day happen to North and South Korea.

Sociologists have found the decay of culture and decline of social cohesiveness in conjunction with the rise of a periphery culture to be the primary cause of the disintegration of many groups.[90] Cultural vitality and social cohesion play an immense role in the long-term success of a people. Charles Darwin wrote in *The Descent of Man*, 1871:

> A tribe including many members who, from possessing in a high degree the spirit of patriotism, fidelity, obedience, courage, and sympathy, were always ready to aid one another, and to sacrifice themselves for the common good, would be victorious over most other tribes. [91]

Culture is one of the most potent and poorly understood forces on the planet. Like the air we breathe, it is essential but remains unnoticed until it fails. Culture affects our attitudes, choices, and actions. It affects our interactions with others' abilities to lead and be led, work in teams, and win. It affects the effectiveness of all levels of human organization.

The Path of Fitness

Some cultures steadily improve the lives of increasing numbers of a population better than other ones. This steady improvement of a people I call "the Path of Fitness."

> **The Path of Fitness** is the collection of perspectives and practices that cause a people to flourish by steadily increasing the proportion of the population that have (a) healthy diets and clean water, (b) adequate clothing and other necessities,

(c) individual, marital, and family rights, (d) quality healthcare, (e) desirable choices regarding residency, education, and occupation, (f) safe and advantageous employment, (g) sustainable lifestyles, and (h) three-generation life expectancies.

Before the 1960s, the U.S. culture, for the most part, moved us along on the Path of Fitness. It steadily increased the proportion of people who enjoyed the benefits listed above. Not everything was perfect. Women and minorities needed to be included more, and we needed to live more sustainably. These deficiencies needed correcting, but otherwise we were on the Path of Fitness.

Cultural Relativism

Cultural Relativism, a concept found in anthropology and sociology and widely accepted in most academic institutions, is a worldview that has slowed our progress.

> **Cultural Relativism** is the idea that no culture is inherently better than another, and no one has a basis to judge the perspectives and practices of people of other cultures.

The fact is that some cultures convey fitness and well-being to their people, move them along the Path of Fitness, and persist through time better than other ones. In this sense, some cultures are better than others.

While cultural relativism makes people feel good and furthers intercultural harmony, it suspends critical judgments. For example, clearly the cultures and countries of Haiti and North Korea are not as desirable as those of Switzerland, Singapore, or South Korea. Viewing all cultures as equally desirable is like viewing all student work as equally meritorious. Not making distinctions between sloppy and well-organized work, factually correct and incorrect work, and dysfunctional and functional negatively affects learning, and not making distinctions between cultures that move along the path of fitness and those that do not negatively affects people's well-being. To be effective, successful, and persist through time, we must make qualitative distinctions between winning and losing practices and teach our children to make them.

So how do we further cultural harmony and distinguish between winning and losing perspectives and practices? We let others—who mean us no harm and do not infringe on our freedoms—be. Then, we critically examine our own and others' perspectives and practices, reject and stigmatize the counterproductive ones, and support and adopt the ones that yield predominately positive effects.

Today, half a century after the cultural relativism nonsense started, living standards have stagnated, American influence has declined, many more of our citizens are struggling, and a smaller proportion of our population have acquired a full complement of Winning Perspectives and Practices.

Winning Practices

If we study science, we learn that scientists have formulated few laws and they do not view any of the laws as absolutes. The few laws found in science only qualify as laws as substantial empirical evidence supports them, no contradictory evidence disputes them, and the relationships they describe hold throughout the universe. When new observations contradict established laws, scientists reformulate the laws.

Similarly, few practices qualify as Winning Practices, and we should not view the ones that do as absolutes. Viewing a practice as a convention or one of many possibilities is superior to seeing it as "the right way" to do something. This may not be apparent when we are young and have not traveled much, but it becomes apparent as we gain experience. There are many ways to do something. Our approaches are merely a subset of a larger set of possibilities. They may or may not be the best ones. Thus, we should only prefer our practices until we find better ones.

Viewing our approaches in this manner is superior to viewing them as the right ways of doing things because it conveys temporariness and openness to change, which in turn facilitates adaptation, improvement, and fitness. Just as avoiding certitude in science facilitates the development of more accurate theories and laws, avoiding certitude in our daily lives facilitates our adaptation and improvement.

Another challenge with our approaches is that people evaluate their desirability differently. Most people care more about a practice's short-term effects on themselves or their group. Few people think about the effects of their practices on others, on the environment, and in the long term. For example, it may be a best practice for some people to refuse to work overtime. They may have all the money they need, so being home to perform household duties and/or parent their children are better uses of their time. However, from the standpoint of their employers and colleagues, their decision to refuse overtime is not a best practice. Rather, the best practice when the interests of employers, colleagues, and family members are considered may be to inform their employers that they prefer not to work overtime but that they will work overtime when it is critical to the business.

We may consider buying a new car, taking good care of it, and keeping it for several years to be a best practice. It eliminates the risk of acquiring an unreliable form of transportation associated with purchasing used cars, and it costs less than buying a new car and selling it every two to three years. However, this practice may not be a best one in the long term when we have limited credit and need to borrow money to purchase the car. The additional financing costs and debt may more negatively affect our lives during an economic downturn than would an occasional problem with a quality used car.

To counter these limitations, I developed the concept of Winning Practices. Winning Practices take more time to identify and develop but generate fewer negative effects. They consider a practice's effects in five ways: (1) on the individual, (2) on the group, (3) on the environment, (4) in the short term, and (5) in the long term.

Collegial improvement is one of some two hundred Winning Practices that I discuss in the *Flourish* Series. Collegial improvement comes from the observation that conservatives, moderates, and progressives all add value to the improvement process. Progressives identify potentially advantageous changes and push for their implementation. Conservatives defend the status quo and identify the adverse effects of changes. Moderates, at their best, pilot the proposed changes, examine the effects, mitigate any negative ones, and support the changes that *prove* advantageous. Collegial improvement is a Winning Practice because we obtain fairer, more effective, and more widely supported outcomes for individuals, the larger group, and the environment in the short- and long-term when we use it to create institutions, laws, and polices.

The prevalence or absence of Winning Practices in a population determines whether its people flourish, decline, or subsist. We align our lives with Winning Practices, or we forgo their positive effects. We convey Winning Practices to our citizens, or we lose the benefits they bring to our institutions, enterprises, and governments.

Winning Practices—actions that positively affect individuals, groups, and/or the environment in the short- and long-term.

CHAPTER 12

Toward Truth, Freedom, Fitness, and Decency

If we make up our minds that this is a drab and purposeless universe, it will be that, and nothing else. On the other hand, if we believe that the earth is ours, and that the sun and moon hang in the sky for our delight, there will be joy upon the hills and gladness in the fields, because the Artist in our souls glorifies creation. Surely, it gives dignity to life to believe we are born into this world for noble ends, and that we have a higher destiny than can be accomplished within the narrow limits of this physical life.[92]

—Helen Keller

Our lives depend on a habitable planet, territory, resources, a larger community, a home, a workplace, parents, a healthy set of genes, other family members, and friends. Beyond these things, our lives depend on Winning Perspectives and Practices.

Winning Perspectives describe our context. They suggest our means and end, as well as a need for an aspirational philosophy of life aligned with reality, nature, and human nature. Winning Perspectives help us identify Winning Practices.

The Winning Perspectives and our history suggest that Truth, Freedom, Fitness, and Decency are four of the most crucial Winning Perspectives and Practices.

Truth accurately approximates reality, natural processes, and depictions of current and past events.

Freedom is the ability to fulfill our needs, think, speak, associate, travel, work, marry, have children as we choose, author our lives, and actualize.

Fitness is the ability of organisms to flourish, procure resources, reproduce, and flourish relative to other organisms.

Decency involves treating others who mean us no harm with respect and consideration and as we want them to treat us.

Truth enables us to understand our context, trust one another, and work together. Freedom allows us to author our lives. Our initial perceptions are only a start in the quest for truth. Fitness is the underlying aim of life. Our freedoms end where others' freedoms start. Decency endears us to others, enables us to work with others, and furthers specialization, trade, win-wins, and synergy. Together, Truth, Freedom, Fitness, and Decency enable us to multiply our strength to persist through time.

Our most potent understanding of truth comes from science, our sense of freedom comes from our American founders, our need for fitness from evolution, and our sense of decency from our Judeo-Christian heritage.

Fitness is our end. Truth, Freedom, and Decency are our noble means. Devotion to them gives our lives meaning. They further our effectiveness and well-being. They help us bridge the cultural divide.

The thirty-six Winning Practices that I discuss in a subsequent book delineate how we flourish in our context. They address the individual, family, education, enterprise, and government, and they compose an unusually practical approach to life that aligns with reality, nature, and human nature. Figure 10 lists the thirty-six overarching Winning Practices and Appendix D all the Winning Practices discussed in the *Flourish* Series.

Helen Keller was the first *blind, deaf, and mute* person to earn a Bachelor of Arts degree. She was also an accomplished author, political activist, and lecturer. It's hard for us to imagine her early life and all she overcame. It is also hard for us to fathom the difference her life has made in the lives of all subsequent handicapped people.

It would have been easy for Helen Keller to find her life meaningless, but her parents and teacher Anne Sullivan had other ideas. They sought to free Helen Keller from her handicaps. And so it is for us: Although we find no intent in nature, as perceptive, thinking, able, imaginative social beings, we may fill our lives with intent and meaning "beyond the narrow limits of this life." The Winning Perspectives and Practices help us do this. They not only describe our context and what matters, but they reveal how we may flourish and persist!

Figure 10:
Winning Practices of a Free, Fit, and Prosperous People

Individual

Health

Thought

Integrity

Proactivity

Excellence

Thrift and Investment

Family

Spouse Selection

Marriage

Responsible Parenting

Empowering Habit Formation

Group

Affiliation

Decency

Understanding

Leadership

Teamwork

Improvement

Education

Research and Knowledge

Education and Life Preparation

Parental Choice

Results-Oriented Education

Enterprise

Free Enterprise and Markets

Responsible Corporate Governance

Prudent Regulation

Enterprise Competitiveness

Government

Government of the People

Powers, Prohibitions, and Structure

Freedoms, Rights, and Responsibilities

The Rule of Law

Inclusion and Meritocracy

Prudent Taxation

Financial Strength

Social Safety Nets

Consumer-Driven Healthcare

Assimilation

Peace through Fitness

Sustainability

Acknowledgments

It is impossible to name all the people who directly and indirectly influenced my thinking. Included are some of the greatest leaders, thinkers, explorers, and innovators in history. Their thoughts and work enable us to realize the best of what life offers. The Appendix C and endnotes provide the names of many of these people.

Though many people have provided feedback to me concerning the content of this series, their mention here does not mean that they endorse the perspectives and practices in it. I am solely responsible for its content.

In the preparation of this book, I thank my beautiful and ever supportive wife, Leokadia; my sons, Karl and Asher; daughters-in-law, Kristi and Kalee; and my extraordinary mother and father. I would like to thank my faithful and talented administrative assistant, Sherri Woods; insightful and encouraging editor, Deborah Grandinetti; patient and wise publicists, Jane Wesman and Felecia Sinusas; energetic and able social media publicist, Autumn Glading; exceptional graphic artist, Patty Schuster; photographer, Michelle Reed; and the brave and thoughtful members of my advisory board, Susannah Adelson, Roxanne Parmele, Barb Quijano, and Russ Smith. I also want to thank Justin Branch, Rachael Brandenburg, Elizabeth Brown, Karen Cakebread, Elizabeth Chenette, Steven Elizalde, Jen Glynn, Tanya Hall, Jay Hodges, Carrie Jones, AprilJo Murphy, Pam Nordberg, and Chelsea Richards of Greenleaf Book Group.

I thank longtime friends and supporters Hy Ackerman, Rolly Anderson, Bill Burrows, Joe Coleman, John Doyle, Evan Dreyfuss, Brian Dunsirn, Bill Ellis, Tom Ewert, Verne Freeman, Dan Fisher, Had Fuller, Jim Howe, Michael Korchmar, Ken and Amy Lockhard, Steve McMahon, Jean Merrell, Carole-Ann Miller, Mark Nielsen, Rosemary Perez, Steve Pond, Jack Reinelt, Don Strumillo, Leah Romero, Ed Telling, Bob Vanourek, Jennifer Lehmann Weng, Carl Youngman, and Karl Zinsmeister. I thank Jon Carroll, Jim Cohen, Mark Danni, Katherine Davies, Paul de Lima, Tom Embrescia, Gary Fenchuk, Dick Glowacki, Clint Greenleaf, Suzanne Heiligman, Richard, Kaufman, Deborah Keller, Jim Jameson, Steve McConnell, Bill Morton, Dr. Story Musgrave, Lori Ruhlman, Ed Samek, Lindsay Schlauch, Ed Schifman, Mitch Sill, Haisook Somers, and Rollie Strum for their input and/or encouragement.

I thank Bella Stahl and the exceptional team members of CNY Feeds; the dedicated staffs of the Syracuse YMCA, Northwest YMCA, and Florida Nature Conservancy; and the incredible staffs and members of the International YPO-WPO and CEO organizations. I am also appreciative of all the people who spent hours developing Google, Wikipedia, and Wikiquote. Their efforts made finding and recalling information so much easier and ultimately enriched the content of this book immeasurably.

APPENDIX A

Additional Presidential Constitutional Failings

GEORGE H. W. BUSH

Americans with Disabilities Act of 1990

Military Action in Kuwait without a Declaration of War

BILL CLINTON

Family and Medical Leave Act of 1993

The Brady Handgun Violence Prevention Act of 1993

The Violent Crime Control and Law Enforcement Act of 1994

Use of the Line Item Veto, Which Is Unconstitutional

Deployment of the U.S. Military 41 Times around the World

Sodomization of a White House Intern and Untruthful Testimony

Additional Supreme Court Constitutional Failings

Home Building & Loan Association v. Blaisdell (1934) enabled governments to interfere with contracts between private parties.[93]

Helvering v. Davis (1937) gave Congress the green light to redistribute wealth. It gave Congress a free hand to legislate without judicial review.[94]

United States v. Carolene Products (1938) enabled federal and state governments to pass legislation that significantly devalues property without compensating the owners. It enabled the government to infringe upon citizen and enterprise economic liberties without judicial review.[95]

Wickard v. Filburn (1942) extended the federal regulatory authority to nearly every productive economic activity. It enabled the federal government to regulate economic activities that were not interstate and not commerce. It ended the principle that the federal government only has the powers expressly granted to it in the Constitution.[96]

Chevron U.S.A. v. Natural Resources Defense Council (1984) gave the departments and agencies of the Executive branch the power to interpret the law.[97]

Bennis v. Michigan (1996) gave the government the authority to seize the property of innocent people without judicial hearings.[98]

Whitman v. American Trucking Associations (2001) enabled Congress to pass poorly defined laws and let unelected regulatory agencies fill in the details.[99]

Grutter v. Bollinger (2003) gave institutions the right to use racial preferences in their admittance procedures.[100]

Kelo v. City of New London (2005) gave governments the right to use eminent domain to take private property for economic development.[101]

Special Sources

Giants

The Ten Commandments	Moses
The Art of War	Sun Tzu
The Apology of Socrates	Plato
The New Oxford Annotated Bible with the Apocrypha	
Ninety-Five Theses; Catechisms; Lecture on the Papacy; On Temporal Authority	Martin Luther
The Principia[a]	Isaac Newton
The Declaration of Independence	Thomas Jefferson
An Inquiry into the Nature and Causes of the Wealth of Nations	Adam Smith
The Pennsylvania Constitution of 1776	Benjamin Franklin et al
The Constitution of the United States of America and the Bill of Rights	Hamilton, Madison, Morris, Washington et al
The Federalist Papers	Hamilton, Jay, Madison
On the Origin of Species	Charles Darwin
General Relativity; Special Relativity[b]	Albert Einstein
I Have a Dream	Martin Luther King, Jr.
Lee Kuan Yew: The Grand Master's Insights on China, The United States, and the World[c]	Lee Kuan Yew

Significant

Berkshire Hathaway Annual Reports	Warren Buffett
The 7 Habits of Highly Effective People	Stephen Covey
Principles	Ray Dalio
Life Evolving	Christian de Duve
A Universe of Consciousness	Gerald Edelman
Capitalism and Freedom; Free to Choose	Milton Friedman
Jews, Confucians, and Protestants	Lawrence Harrison
Cosmos; Dragons of Eden; The Demon-Haunted World	Carl Sagan
Winning[d]	Jack and Suzy Welch
Ants; On Human Nature; Consilience; The Future of Life	E. O. Wilson

Very Helpful

As a Man Thinketh	James Allen
Big History	Benjamin, Brown, Christian
The Little Book of Common Sense Investing	John Bogle
The One Minute Manager	Blanchard, Johnson
How to Win Friends and Influence People	Dale Carnegie
The Richest Man in Babylon	George Clason
Good to Great	Jim Collins
Aerobics	Kenneth Cooper
Algorithms to Live By	Christian and Griffiths
Jews, God, and History	Max Dimont
Leadership Is an Art	Max DePree
The Power of Habit	Charles Duhigg
Civilization: The West and the Rest	Niall Ferguson
Common Sense Economics	Gwartney, Lee, Stroup
Sapiens; Homo Deus	Yuval Noah Harari
Dune; Dune Messiah; Children of Dune	Frank Herbert
How the Scots Invented the Modern World	Arthur Herman
Culture and Organizations	Hofstede, Hofstede, Minkov
Men Are from Mars, Women Are from Venus	John Gray
Being There	Erica Komisar
Life Ascending	Nick Lane
9 Presidents Who Screwed Up America	Brion McClanahan
The Dirty Dozen	Levey and Mellor
The Road Less Traveled	M. Scott Peck
Brand Luther	Andrew Pettegree
The Chosen; My Name is Asher Lev	Chaim Potok
Our Kids	Robert Putnam
The 5000 Year Leap	Cleon Skousen
Nature's Fortune	Adams, Tercek
The Outsiders	William Thorndike, Jr.
How Children Succeed	Paul Tough

[a] *The Clockwork Universe*, Edward Dolnick
[b] *Einstein*, Walter Isaacson
[c] By Allison and Blackwill
[d] By Jack and Suzy Welch

Summary of *Toward Truth, Freedom, Fitness, and Decency*

Losing Our Way
Inclusion Failures
The Change in the Election of U.S. Senators
Presidential Constitutional Failings
Supreme Court Constitutional Failings
Special Interest Government
Less Faith-Community Relevance
Less Integrity, Responsibility, and Civility
Promiscuity and the Decline of Marriage
Poorly Parented Children
Unionization of Education
Liberalization of Education
Social Justice Missteps
Cultural Relativism, Nonjudgmentalism, Multiculturalism
Declining Discipline, Poor Habits, and Less Learning
Oligopoly and Monopoly
Offshoring
Entitlement
Consumerism and Debt
Easy Money
Hubris and Nation-Building
Immigration Failures
Distorted News
Political Polarization
Separation from Nature

Winning Perspectives
Singapore, Switzerland, and the United States
Country Characteristics
Winning Perspectives

Truth

Causality
Fallacy, Correlation, Necessity, and Sufficiency
The Inanimate and Animate Worlds

Scale

Evolution
Competition
Comparative Advantage
Natural Selection

Gradualism
Interrelated

Fitness
Meritocracy
Procreation
The Underlying Aim of Life

Human Nature
Individual
Familial
Social
Superorganisms
Environmental Alignment

Periodic Disaster

Eco-Dependency
Externality

Winning Perspective Summary

Winning Practices
Individual
Family
Group
Education
Enterprise
Government
Culture
The Path of Fitness
Cultural Relativism
Winning Practices

Toward Truth, Freedom, Fitness, Decency
Truth
Freedom
Fitness
Decency

Appendix A: Presidential Constitutional Failings
Appendix B: Supreme Court Constitutional Failings
Appendix C: Special Sources
Appendix D: Concepts, Perspectives, and Practices

APPENDIX E

Summary of *Winning Practices of a Free, Fit, and Prosperous People*

Winning Perspectives
Singapore, Switzerland, and the United States
Country Characteristics
Winning Perspectives

Winning Practices
Individual
Family
Groups
Education
Enterprise
Government
Levels of Human Organization
Culture
The Path of Fitness
Cultural Relativism
Winning Practices

Health
Hygiene
Nutrition
Periodic Fasting
Sleep
Exercise
Avoiding Harm
Medical and Dental Care
DNA Fidelity
Reflection
Purpose and Social Interaction
Balance

Thought
Assimilation
Visualization
Creativity
Reverse Engineering
Research

Choice and Alignment
Focus
Rehearsal
Mentors

Integrity
Truthfulness
Honorableness
Reliability
The Effects Test

Proactivity
Responsibility
Constructive Speech and Action
Empowering Habit Formation
Purpose
Preparation
Work
Fitness-Related Service

Excellence
Extra Thought, Focus, Effort, and Time
High Standards, Attention to Detail, Improvement,
Near-Perfect Practice, and Perseverance
Facilitators and Impediments

Thrift and Investment
Minimizing Expenditures
Automated Savings
Financial Tools and Investments
Rule of 69
Present Value and Future Value
Present and Future Value of an Annuity
Investment
Advantageously Buying and Selling Assets
Minimizing Taxes
The Keys to Wealth

Spouse Selection
Differences between Men and Women
Vetted Love
Deferred Sex
Necessary Attributes
Family Decision-Making

Marriage
Love and Accommodation
Specialization
Commitment and Fidelity

Responsible Parenting
Progeny Consciousness
Nurture and Discipline
Unconditional Love
Self-Control
Deferred Gratification
Self-Discipline
Conscientiousness and Discipline
The Keys to Discipline
Literacy and Education
Experiences and Challenges
Lifelong Role Models

Empowering Habit Formation
Forming Empowering Habits
Habits—Cues, Routines, Rewards, Cravings
Keystone Habits
Habits of Individual and Group Effectiveness
Breaking Debilitating Habits

Affiliation
Accountability
Attendance
Punctuality
Appearance
Congeniality
Independent Thought
Friendship

Decency
Ally Acquisition
Respectfulness
Consideration and Appreciation
The Modified Golden Rule
Apology and Forgiveness
Expenditure of Time, Energy, Resources

Understanding
Humility
Trust
The Emotional Bank Account
Listening
Clarification
Shared Experience

Leadership
Practices of Individual Effectiveness
Practices of Group Effectiveness
Mission, Vision, Plans
Stakeholder Inclusion
Assignments
Goals
Incentives
Evaluations
Structure, Strategy, Execution
Cultures of Success
Good Decisions
Realism, Courage, Assertiveness
Passion and Perseverance

Teamwork
Initiative, Strong Ties, and Weak Ties
Practices of Individual Effectiveness
Practices of Group Effectiveness
Leadership Selection and Retention
Member Selection and Retention
Positive Diversity
Equal Opportunity, Meritocracy, Rewards
Win-Win
Cooperation, Specialization, Synergy
Associations

Improvement
Winning Practices
Competition
Innovation
Pilots
Sustainability
Continuous Improvement
Collegial Improvement

Knowledge
The Scientific Method
Libraries and Databases
An Education, Research, Extension System
A Free and Responsible Press
Conflict of Interest Avoidance

Universal Education
Parent Accountability
Student Accountability
Real-World Feedback
Empowering Habit Formation
Life- and Science-Based Curriculum
Elementary Curriculum
Seven Secondary Tracks
Homogenous Grouping
Individualized Learning

Parental Choice
Equitable and Diverse County Districts
Ending the Public Education Monopoly
An Island of Socialism
Parental Choice
State Goals and Exams

Results-Oriented Education
Benchmarking
Administration Empowerment and Accountability
Principal-Teacher Empowerment and Accountability
How Children Succeed
Bridging Conservative and Liberal Biases

Free Enterprise and Markets
Private Property
Free Enterprise
Corporations
Public Goods
Profit
Free Markets
Free Trade
Comparative Advantage
Capital Formation and Investment

Responsible Corporate Governance
Stakeholder Inclusion
Independent and Stakeholder Directors
Media Reports of Corporate Misconduct
Winning Cultures

Prudent Regulation
Contract Enforcement
Transparency
Market Share Restrictions
Leverage Restrictions
Externality Taxation
Do No Harm
Long-Term Incentives

Enterprise Competitiveness
Customer Focus
A Performance and Improvement Culture
Minimal Overhead
Limited Leverage
Willing and Able Workforce
Well-Developed Public Infrastructure
Minimal Government Burdens

Problems with Democracies
Human Fallibility
Conflicts of Interest
Special Interests
Lack of Accountability
Representatives Play Santa Claus
Leaders Love Power
Short-Term and Group Thinking
Majorities Dominate Minorities

Government of the People
A Constitution
Dispersing and Checking Power
A Republic with a Bicameral Legislature
Double and Triple Supermajorities

Powers, Prohibitions, and Structure
Specified Federal Powers
Prohibitions
Legislative, Executive, and Judicial Branches
The House
The Senate
The Executive Council
The Supreme Court

Freedoms, Rights, and Responsibilities
Freedoms
Rights
Responsibilities
Citizenship Qualifications
Voter Qualifications
Weighting the Votes of Parents

The Rule of Law
Constitutional, Understood, Widely Supported
Collegial Improvement
Legislatively Originated
Piloted, Beneficial, and Stakeholder-Oriented
Impartially and Consistently Applied to All
Justice
Periodic Review
Judicious Litigation

Inclusion and Meritocracy
Ethnic Sensitivity and Appreciation
Integration
Meritocracy and Comparative Advantage
Equal Opportunity
Goldilocks Minimum Wages
A Can-Do Attitude

Prudent Taxation
Disincentivize the Undesirables
Sales Taxes on Nonessentials
The Uniform Application of Taxes
Taxing and Spending Restraints
The Federal Reserve
Monetary Policy
Inflation
Short-Term Business Cycle

Deflation
Long-Term Business Cycle
Sound Lending Practices
Balanced Budgets and Limited Indebtedness
Prudent Taxation, Productivity, Full Employment
Fiscal Policy
Productivity
Capital Formation

Social Safety Nets
Avoiding Socialism and the Redistribution of Wealth
Incentivized Savings Accounts
State Social Safety Nets
Employee Insurances

Consumer-Driven Healthcare
Advantageous Immigration and Judicious Litigation
Goldilocks Minimum Wages and Savings Accounts
Universal Coverage
Patient Choice
Out-of-Pocket Payments

Assimilation
From Many, One
United We Stand, Divided We Fall
English as the National Language
Impervious Borders
Advantageous Immigration

Peace through Fitness
Seven Levels of Human Fitness
Financial Strength
Law Enforcement and Justice
Military, Cyber, Intelligence Strength and Restraint
Allies
Limited Treaty Powers
Democratic Realism

Sustainability
Fresh Water, Air, Land, and Ocean Quality
Ecosystem and Biodiversity Conservation
Resource Use, Recycling, and Waste Disposal
Clean Energy
Prudent Growth

Endnotes

1. Niall Ferguson, *Civilization: The West and the Rest*, The Penguin Press, New York, 2011, 5.

2. Alexander Hamilton, James Madison, and John Jay, *The Federalist Papers*, No. 45, Edited by Clinton Rossiter, Signet Classics, New York, 2003, 289.

3. Gerhard Peters and John T. Woolley, "Executive Orders." *The American Presidency Project*, Edited by John T. Woolley and Gerhard Peters, Santa Barbara, California, 1999–2018, http://www.presidency.ucsb.edu/data/orders.php and "Executive Orders Disposition Tables: Franklin D. Roosevelt," *Federal Register*, https://www.archives.gov/federal-register/executive-orders/roosevelt.html and "Executive Orders Disposition Tables: Lyndon B. Johnson," *Federal Register*, https://www.archives.gov/federal-register/executive-orders/johnson.html and "Executive Orders Disposition Tables: George W. Bush," *Federal Register*, https://www.archives.gov/federal-register/executive-orders/wbush.html.

4. "Obama Encourages Illegals," *The Washington Times*, Washington, DC, November 18, 2009, http://www.washingtontimes.com/news/2009/nov/18/obama-encourages-illegals/.

5. Brion McClanahan, *9 Presidents Who Screwed Up America*, Regnery History, Washington, DC, 2016, 172.

6. Brion McClanahan, 274.

7. James Madison, "Speech at the Virginia Convention to ratify the Federal Constitution," June 6, 1788, *Debates in the Several State Conventions on the Adoption of the Federal Constitution*, Edited by Jonathan Elliot, J. B. Lippincott, Philadelphia, 1836, v. 3, 87.

8. James Madison, "Letter to James Robertson," April 20, 1831, https://en.wikisource.org/wiki/James_Madison_letter_to_James_Robertson.

9. Carol Tucker, "The 1950s—Powerful Years for Religion," USC News, June 16, 1997, https://news.usc.edu/25835/The-1950s-Powerful-Years-for-Religion/, and Kelly Shattuck, "7 Startling Facts: An Up Close Look at Church Attendance in America," Church Leaders, Articles for Pastors, November 2015, http://www.churchleaders.com/pastors/pastor-articles/139575-7-startling-facts-an-up-close-look-at-church-attendance-in-america.html.

10. National Institute on Alcohol Abuse and Alcoholism, http://www.niaaa.nih.gov/alcohol-health/overview-alcohol-consumption/alcohol-facts-and-statistics.

11. National Institute on Drug Abuse, "National Survey of Drug Use and Health," http://www.drug abuse.gov/national/-survey-drug-use-health.

12. American Sexual Health Association, "Statistics," http://www.ashasexualhealth.org/stdsstis/statistics/.

13. American Safety Council, SafeMotorist.com, "Aggressive Driving and Road Rage," http://www.safemotorist.com/articles/road_rage.aspx.

14. Transparency International, "World Corruption Perception Index," 2014, https://www.transparency.org/cpi2014/results.

15. NUMBEO, "Crime Index for Country, 2015 Mid-Year," http://www.numbeo.com/crime/rankings_by_country.jsp.

16. Julissa Cruz, "Marriage: More than a Century of Change," Bowling Green State University, Bowling Green, Ohio, 2013, https://www.bgsu.edu/content/dam/BGSU/college-of-arts-and-sciences/NCFMR/documents/FP/FP-13-13.pdf.

17. Robert Putman, *Our Kids: The American Dream in Crisis*, Simon & Schuster, New York, 2015, 62–63.

18. Robert Putman, 69–70.

19. Robert Putman, 78–79.

20. David Brooks, "The Cost of Relativism," *The International New York Times*, March 11, 2015, 8.

21. Lee Kuan Yew, *Lee Kuan Yew: The Grand Master's Insights on China, The United States, and the World*, Graham Alison and Robert D. Blackwill, The MIT Press, Cambridge, 2013, 34.

22. U.S. Federal Reserve, "Outstanding Debt by Sector," www.federalreserve.gov.

23. U.S. Bureau of Labor Statistics, "Employment," www.bls.gov.

24. FRED, Economic Research, Federal Reserve Bank of St. Louis, "U.S. Treasury securities held by the Federal Reserve: All Maturities," https://fred.stlouisfed.org/series/TREAST.

25. Pew Research Center, http://www.pewhispanic.org/2015/09/28/modern-immigration-wave-brings-59-million-to-u-s-driving-population-growth-and-change-through-2065/.

26. World Bank, "GDP per capita, Current U.S. Dollars," https://data.worldbank.org/indicator/NY.GDP.PCAP.CD?end=2015&start=1960.

27. Central Intelligence Agency of the United States, The World Factbook, 2017, https://www.cia.gov/library/publications/the-world-factbook/rankorder/2004rank.html#sn (Note the source indicates that the ranking is for 2017 even though the link has "2004rank" in it.)

28. Central Intelligence Agency of the United States, The World Factbook, 2015, https://www.cia.gov/library/publications/the-world-factbook.

29. Cato Institute, "The Human Freedom Index," 2015, http://www.cato.org/human-freedom-index and "Economic Freedom of the World Rank," 2013, http://www.cato.org/economic-freedom-world/map.

30. Central Intelligence Agency of the United States, The World Factbook, 2016 https://www.cia.gov/library/publications/the-world-factbook.

31. Wikipedia, "List of Countries by Home Ownership Rate," 2013–14, https://en.wikipedia.org/wiki/List_of_countries_by_home_ownership_rate.

32. Transparency International, "World Corruption Index 2014," https://www
.transparency.org/cpi2014/results.

33. World Bank Economic Indicators, 2012, https://data.worldbank.org/indicator/.

34. Wikipedia, "List by Countries by Incarceration Rate," last edited 2018, https://
en.wikipedia.org/wiki/List_of_countries_by_incarceration_rate.

35. Calculated using data from the Central Intelligence Agency of the United States,
The World Factbook, 2015, https://www.cia.gov/library/publications/the-world
-factbook, and International Monetary Fund, 2015, https://www.imf.org/external
/np/sta/ir/IRProcessWeb/data/sgp/eng/cursgp.htm; International Monetary Fund,
2015, https://www.imf.org/external/np/sta/ir/IRProcessWeb/data/che/eng/curche
.htm; International Monetary Fund, 2015, http://www.imf.org/external/np/sta/ir
/IRProcessWeb/data/usa/eng/curusa.htm#I.

36. World Bank Economic Indicators, 2012, https://data.worldbank.org/indicator/.

37. Wikipedia, "Divorce Demography," https://en.wikipedia.org/wiki
/Divorce_demography.

38. Populations decrease in size when fertility rates are below 2.1, World Bank
Economic Indicators, 2014, http://databank.worldbank.org/data/reports
.aspx?source=world-development-indicators#.

39. World Bank Economic Indicators, 2014, https://data.worldbank.org/indicator/.

40. Central Intelligence Agency of the United States, The World Factbook, 2008, https://
www.cia.gov/library/publications/the-world-factbook/rankorder/2228rank.html.

41. Wikipedia, 2015, "Universal Health Coverage by Country," https://en.wikipedia
.org/wiki/Universal_health_coverage_by_country.

42. World Bank Economic Indicators, 2012, https://data.worldbank.org/indicator/.

43. World Bank Economic Indicators, 2012, https://data.worldbank.org/indicator/.

44. OECD, "Education at a Glance," 2014, http://www.oecd.org/edu/Education
-at-a-Glance-2014.pdf, 41; Wikipedia, "Education in Singapore," 2012, https://
en.wikipedia.org/wiki/Education_in_Singapore.

45. Wikipedia, "Education in Singapore," 2012, https://en.wikipedia.org/wiki
/Education_in_Singapore, and "Researcher's Report 2014 Country Profile:
Switzerland," Deloitte, 4, http://ec.europa.eu/euraxess/pdf/research_policies
/country_files/Switzerland_Country_Profile_RR2014_FINAL.pdf.

46. World Bank Economic Indicators, 2014, https://data.worldbank.org/indicator/.

47. World Bank Economic Indicators, 2015, https://data.worldbank.org/indicator/.

48. World Bank Economic Indicators, 1960; Central Intelligence Agency of the
United States, The World Fact Book, 2016, https://www.cia.gov/library
/publications/the-world-factbook.

49. World Bank Economic Indicators, 2010, https://data.worldbank.org/indicator/.

50. World Bank Economic Indicators, 2010, https://data.worldbank.org/indicator/.

51. Encyclopedia.com, Jack Welch, http://www.encyclopedia.com/topic/Jack_Welch.aspx.

52. Jack Welch, *Jack Straight from the Gut*, Warner Books, New York, 2001, 4.

53. Winston Churchill, Speech in the House of Commons, *Royal Assent*, HC Deb 17 May 1916, v. 82, cc 1578.

54. Dale Carnegie, *How to Stop Worrying and Start Living*, "Thomas Edison," Pocket Books, Kindle eBook, August 24, 2010, 36.

55. Carl Sagan, "Wonder and Skepticism," *Skeptical Enquirer*, Volume 19.1, January/ February 1995.

56. Carl Sagan, *The Demon-Haunted World: Science as a Candle in the Dark*, Ballantine Books, New York, 1996, 28.

57. Will Durant, *The Story of Civilization, Volume 1: Our Oriental Heritage*, Simon & Schuster, New York, 1954; 263–264.

58. Annie Dillard, *Pilgrim at Tinker Creek*, Bantam Books, Inc., New York, 1975; 9–10.

59. Wikipedia, "Abiogenesis," http://en.wikpedia.org/wiki/Abiogenesis.

60. Wikipedia, "Abiogenesis."

61. Wikipedia, "Timeline of Evolutionary History of Life," http://en.wikpedia.org /wiki/Timeline_of_evolutionary_history_of_life.

62. Rachel Brazil, "Hydrothermal Vents and the Origins of Life," ChemistryWorld .com, April 16, 2017, https://www.chemistryworld.com/feature/hydrothermal -vents-and-the-origins-of-life/3007088.article.

63. Wikipedia, "Evolution," http://en.wikipedia.org/wiki/Evolution.

64. Wikipedia, "Timeline of the Evolution of Life," http://en.wikpedia.org/wiki /Timeline_of_evolutionary_history_of_life.

65. Wikipedia, "Evolution," http://en.wikipedia.org/wiki/Evolution.

66. Wikipedia, "Timeline of the Evolution of Life," http://en.wikipedia.org/wiki /Timeline_of_evolutionary_history_of_life.

67. Wikipedia, "Timeline of the Evolution of Life."

68. Charles Darwin, *On the Origin of Species*, 1859, 61.

69. Wikipedia, "Origin of the Domestic Dog," https://en.wikipedia.org/wiki /Origin_of_the_domestic_dog.

70. E. O. Wilson, *On Human Nature*, Harvard University Press, Cambridge, 1978, 88.

71. Will Durant, "The Map of Human Character," Lecture broadcast over WGN, Chicago, November 18, 1945, http://www.theimaginativeconservative .org/2012/05/map-of-human-character.html.

72. Wikipedia, "Total Fertility Rate," http://en.wikipedia.org/wiki/Total_fertility_rate, "United States."

73. Jared Diamond, *Guns, Germs, and Steel*, W. W. Norton, New York, Kindle eBook, April 17, 1999, 429.

74. Thomas Jefferson, "The Declaration of Independence of the United States of America," *The Declaration of Independence and the Constitutions of the United States of America*, Cato Institute, Washington DC, 9–10.

75. E. O. Wilson, *On Human Nature*, Harvard University Press, Cambridge, 1978, 84.

76. Robert Wright, *The Moral Animal: Why We Are the Way We Are: The New Science of Evolutionary Psychology*, Vintage Books, New York, 1995, 13.

77. E. O. Wilson, *On Human Nature*, Harvard University Press, Cambridge, 1978, 84.

78. David Brooks, "Social Animal: How the New Sciences of Human Nature Can Help Make Sense of Life," *Annals of Psychology*, January 17, 2011.

79. Wikipedia, "Extinction Events," http://en.wikipedia.org/wiki/Extinction_event.

80. Wikipedia, "World Population," http://en.wikipedia.org/wiki/World_population.

81. Wikipedia, "List of Famines," http://en.wikipedia.org/wiki/List_of_famines.

82. Wikipedia, "List of Famines."

83. Carl Sagan, *Pale Blue Dot: A Vision of the Human Future in Space*, Random House, New York, 1994, 371.

84. Nuclear Energy Institute, http://www.nei.org/Knowledge-Center /Nuclear-Statistics/On-Site-Storage-of-Nuclear-Waste.

85. Norman Myers, *Gaia Atlas of Planet Management*, Anchor, Hamburg, 1992, 159.

86. David Biello, "How Much Is Too Much? Estimating Greenhouse Gas Emissions," *Scientific American*, April 2009.

87. Carl Sagan, *Cosmos: A Personal Voyage*, 1980, Episode 6, 58 min, 56 sec.

88. Geert Hofstede, Gert Jan Hoffstede, and Michael Minkov, *Cultures and Organizations: Software of the Mind*, McGraw-Hill, New York, 2010, 3–12.

89. Geert Hofstede, Gert Jan Hofstede, and Michael Minkov, 12–14.

90. Geert Hofstede, Gert Jan Hofstede, and Michael Minkov, 53–88.

91. Charles Darwin, "Chapter V: On the Development of the Intellectual and Moral Faculties During Primeval and Civilized Times," *The Descent of Man*, 1871, 132, https://en.wikisource.org/wiki/The_Descent_of_Man_(Darwin)/Chapter_V.

92. Helen Keller, "Dreams That Come True," *Personality*, American Foundation for the Blind, December 1927.

93. Robert Levy and William Mellor, *The Dirty Dozen: How Twelve Supreme Court Cases Radically Expanded Government and Eroded Freedom*, Cato Institute, Washington DC, 2008, 50–66.

94. Levy and Mellor, 19–36.

95. Levy and Mellor, 181–197.

96. Levy and Mellor, 20–49.

97. Levy and Mellor, 67–85.

98. Levy and Mellor, 143–154.

99. Levy and Mellor, 67–85.

100. Levy and Mellor, 198–214.

101. Levy and Mellor, 155–168.

Index

An *f* following a page number indicates a figure on that page.

presidential constitutional failings
  overview, 12–13, 17–19
  lists of, 14–16f, 129
procreation, 82–87
progressives
  and collegial improvement, 120–21
  and education, 26
  support for social programs, 31–32, 33
promiscuity in the United States, 22–23
public schools, 26
Putnam, Robert, 23, 24

Q

quality of government comparison, 42f, 45–46

R

Reagan, Ronald, 17
religion
  decrease in credibility, 21–23
  science-based beliefs compared to, 3, 4
religious-to-secular transformation, 3–4
rewards, 90, 91, 96
right leaning coalition, 6, 120–21
RNA, sufficient conditions for, 59, 69, 78–79
Roosevelt, Franklin, 12, 13, 14f
Roosevelt, Theodore, 12, 13, 14f, 17

S

Sagan, Carl, 3, 52–54, 106
Sallie Mae and student loans, 33–34
Scale as a Winning Perspective, 63–64, 65f, 66f, 67f, 107
science
  and decrease in credibility of faith-based beliefs, 21–22
  determination of sufficient conditions, 58–61

faith-based beliefs compared to, 3, 4
of human brain, 114
laws and empirical evidence, 119
and our perceptions of the world, 51
perspectives and wisdom within, 38
perspectives from evolution and, 5–6
as source of perspective, 49
study of evolution of life, 71
uncovering invisible causes, 55, 60
and understanding the universe, 53–54, 63–64, 67f
self-centered tendencies, 90
sexual experiences
  cellular traits affected by recombination and sex, 69–70
  childbearing disconnected from marriage, 23
  of children, 24, 86
  cultural practices and evolution, 86–87
  STDs from, 22, 86
sexual reproduction vs. mutations for trait development, 70, 75–76
Shakespeare, William, 81
short-term thinking and tendencies, 90–91, 120
Silent Spring (Carson), 103
Singapore, 41, 44
Singapore, Switzerland, and the United States compared, 41–50
  overview, 41–43, 42f
  competitiveness and income, 48
  country characteristics, 43–44
  education, 47
  family function, 46–47
  freedom and opportunity, 44
  individual well-being, 47
  quality of government, 45–46
  sustainability, 48
Small and Large Distances, 63, 65f
Small and Large Masses, 63, 66f
socialism, 96
social justice missteps, 26–27

About the Author

Mark Bitz is a successful entrepreneur, author, and community leader. Unusually close to nature, well read and traveled, thoughtful, and pragmatic, he is a lifelong student of science, history, culture, government, economics, business, investing, and leadership.

Working his way up from farmhand to president, Mr. Bitz owned and operated Plainville Turkey Farm, Inc., between 1991 and 2007. Under his leadership, the company grew sevenfold and pioneered an all-natural-ingredient deli line, animal-friendly husbandry practices, turkeys grown without antibiotics, and turkeys raised on a vegetarian diet. The company won the American Culinary Institute Best Taste Award, and it was the first turkey company to receive the American Humane Association's "Free Farmed" certification. In 1990, he founded a feed company that he currently owns and operates, and in 2005, he co-founded CNY Crops, Inc., a company that became the largest organic crop operation in the Northeast.

Mr. Bitz has coached youth soccer and basketball. He was instrumental in building the Northwest YMCA in Baldwinsville, New York, and has served on numerous boards. He has chaired the Empire State Young President's Organization, Baldwinsville YMCA, and New York State 4-H Foundation. He has been a director of the Greater Syracuse YMCA, Syracuse Metropolitan Development Association, New York State Business Council, National Turkey Federation, and International Chief Executives Organization. He served on the Cornell Agriculture and Life Science Dean's Advisory Board and the Cornell University Council. Currently, he is a trustee of the Florida Nature Conservancy and vice president of education of the Chief Executives Organization.

Mr. Bitz received his BS in economic development from Purdue University. He was a recipient of the Lehman Fellowship at Cornell, where he received his MS in agricultural economics and completed the coursework and exams toward a PhD in public policy analysis. He has attended numerous Harvard and Oxford executive programs. He was named among the "CNY 40 Under 40" and is the recipient of the Purdue University Alumni of Distinction Award. His turkey business was the Onondaga County Conservation Farm of the Year and the New York State Agricultural Society Business of the Year. He and his wife, Leokadia, have two sons, two daughters-in-law, and two granddaughters.